Developing Excellent Team Leaders

Dick Lynas

author HOUSE®

AuthorHouse™ UK Ltd.
500 Avebury Boulevard
Central Milton Keynes, MK9 2BE
www.authorhouse.co.uk
Phone: 08001974150

First published by AuthorHouse 2/18/2011

ISBN: 978-1-4567-7289-5 (sc)
ISBN: 978-1-4567-7291-8 (dj)
ISBN: 978-1-4567-7290-1 (e)

Cover: Opening day at Taylor High School, New Stevenston, North Lanarkshire, Scotland. August 16, 1982

Contents

About the Author

Dick Lynas is a senior consultant in school leadership and management.

As the first head teacher of a new secondary school in the North Lanarkshire area of Scotland, he was praised by inspectors for the unity of purpose and the caring ethos that he generated among his colleagues. Over the years, that ethos and unity of purpose helped the school to match national statistics for the percentage of pupils achieving university entrance levels, despite the fact that it was situated in the second most deprived council area in Scotland. Dick has long been convinced of the link between leadership development and school improvement and twenty one of the colleagues who served with him during his fifteen years of headship have since gone on to headship – with more waiting in the wings.

Dick became a full-time consultant in school leadership in 1997 and it was in that capacity that he worked with the national development team who were charged in the late 1990s with drawing up a Standard for Headship in Scotland's schools and thereafter developing and delivering the Scottish Qualification for Headship (SQH), a leadership programme that was designed to help aspiring head teachers to achieve that Standard.

In recent years, Dick has focused on developing and delivering a programme based upon the principles that underpin both the SQH and the *Flexible Route to Headship* (FRH) for those who aspire to be team leaders at middle and senior management levels. His programme was included as an example of good practice in the HMIe Report *Leadership for Learning: The challenges of leading in a time of change* (2007). It was also chosen by *Learning Teaching Scotland* as a model of its kind for online trialling as part of the national *Glow* initiative in Scotland.

Away from his profession, Dick devotes a lot of time to planning dream holidays in the sun – even if cannot afford to go on all of them.

Dick can be contacted at dlynas22@aol.com

Acknowledgements

The leadership development programme here presented has evolved over a period of seven years and has benefited from the contributions of many people. In particular, I wish to thank Gillian Hamilton, Quality Improvement Officer in East Ayrshire, Fiona Taylor, Quality Improvement Officer in South Ayrshire and Alison Young, Quality Improvement Officer in North Ayrshire for their constructive comments about the materials over the years.

My own skills as a trainer developed considerably from working with Vivien Casteel, former Head of Staff College in Strathclyde Region, Dr Jenny Reeves, former National Development Officer for the Scottish Qualification for Headship programme and Dr Christine Forde who is Professor of Leadership and Learning at the University of Glasgow.

Mary-Rose Martin, head teacher of Ardrossan Academy in North Ayrshire and an associate HMI, has acted as a tutor on the programme on a number of occasions and has brought her own sharp insights into the demands of school leadership. She also made a number of constructive comments about the early drafts of this book. Mary McLaughlin, CBE, and former head of Notre Dame High School in Glasgow has also contributed her ideas and tutorial skills.

My views about leadership have been influenced over the years by too many writers and too many experiences to mention but I must say that Max de Pree, writer of *Leadership is an Art,* has had a considerable impact on my thinking, as has Peter Drucker in several of his books. References throughout the text and the bibliography convey my debt to many others.

Finally I am happy to acknowledge the value of the feedback from those hundreds of aspiring leaders who have read the materials and participated in the programme over the years, not least in ensuring that it remains relevant to the needs of today's aspiring school leaders.

I shall be happy to correct any copyright issues that I may have overlooked in any future additions.

The cover photograph is from my private collection.

This book is dedicated to my wife Phil

Preface

Preface

Target Audience

Developing Excellent Team Leaders is the course textbook for a programme of leadership development of the same name that is designed, in its two separate versions, to meet the needs of:

- classroom teachers from any sector who aspire to be middle managers or who are newly- appointed middle managers in schools

- serving middle managers who wish to refresh their existing leadership skills or who are interested in a move to senior management in schools.

Outcomes

The overall programme has three outcomes:

- ✓ There will be a *demonstrable* improvement in the quality of learning, teaching and attainment in the area of provision upon which participants choose to focus in their school-based improvement projects

- ✓ There will be a *demonstrable* improvement in the personal leadership skills identified by readers at the start of the programme

- ✓ The school's overall capacity to manage future improvement projects will be *enhanced*

Programme Principles and Structure

The programme is based on the same principles that underpin both the *Scottish Qualification for Headship* programme and the *Flexible Route to Headship* programmes. Overall there is a concern to ensure that the programme combines a proper blend of practice and theory and there is a particular emphasis throughout on the importance of reflection on practice.

More specifically the programme aims to:

- be predominantly practice-based with a focus on leadership development that has an impact on learning outcomes for pupils

- build on experiential learning

- take account of different learning styles of participants

- recognise and explore the importance of personal qualities and interpersonal skills in successful leadership

- promote critical reflection on and analysis of all aspects of leadership and management, particularly leadership development

- acknowledge and utilise, as a key methodology, the power of peer coaching and mentoring in developing self confidence, competence and expertise in leadership and management

- promote critical reading of relevant literature to inform practice

- be subject to formative assessment against a *Standard for Leadership* that is based on *The Standard for Headship*

- meet the criteria for formal recognition of leadership development as defined by the General Teaching Council of Scotland

Based upon the principles outlined above, this leadership development programme comprises *three* integrated elements:

1. The *first* element consists of a *series of workshops* for readers, each of up to two and a half hours duration, inclusive of preparation, and follow-up reflection that extend knowledge and understanding of key school leadership issues. The materials provided in the workshop sessions in this book comprise this first element.

   Each workshop begins with several thought pieces to help readers to think about the leadership issues in focus. These are followed by a brief introduction to the workshop, a list of learning outcomes and a series of activities whereby readers may reflect individually and then with colleagues on how they would handle given leadership challenges as set out in a series of scenarios. Each workshop concludes with a feedback section, in which readers are provided with what previous readers and the world of research have to say about the issues in question and about how they might be handled.

2. The *second* element consists of a follow-up opportunity for readers, with the permission of their head teachers, to draw up a Personal Learning Plan whereby they might contribute to the improvement of some aspect of the school curriculum over a school session while seeking to improve their leadership skills. In this way, readers have the opportunity to apply new leadership knowledge and understanding in real school settings.

3. The *third* element provides readers with an opportunity for readers to construct a *reflective portfolio* in which they evaluate the impact of their improvement project on learning, teaching, attainment and achievement and on personal leadership development. A guide on how to construct a reflective portfolio, with examples, is included later as a support for readers.

Time Line

Readers are encouraged to undertake all aspects of the programme as the combination of theory with practice increases their chances of both *developing* and *applying* their leadership functions and qualities to the benefit of their pupils.

A typical time line of activities to be followed is provided below.

Start point: Undertake the reading and activities associated with the workshops or attend a 1- or 2-day set of workshops based upon the same materials (A popular time to do this is at a suitable point ahead of a new school session)

One month later: Draw up a final action plan for the school-based project and submit for approval to head teacher or to programme coach as appropriate.

Start of school session: Undertake implementation of the action plan over the period of a school session, with email and telephone support from the programme coach available on request.

End of school session: Draw up a reflective portfolio that analyses the leadership challenges that arose during the project, how they were met and what the outcomes were for all involved. Participants then submit this reflective portfolio to the programme coach for formative assessment.

Peer Coaching

As the sub-title of the course textbook implies, there is a strong commitment throughout to the notion of *peer coaching* as a means of developing leadership skills. Modern research indicates that school leaders can learn a great deal by sharing their views and experiences with other colleagues, especially those who have met and overcome similar challenges in similar contexts.

Ideally the workshops that are presented in the pages that follow are intended to promote peer coaching at centrally organised sessions. If for any reason readers are unable to participate in such sessions then it is strongly recommended that they find informal opportunities to share their experiences with like-minded colleagues.

Additional Support

In this connection, the programme writer and coaches are happy to organise face-to-face workshop sessions locally for individual schools and groups of schools and thereafter to provide ongoing personal coaching by phone or email. Alternatively readers may wish to negotiate individual arrangements with one of the programme tutors.

Further details of this extended support and costs are available from:

InfoLeaDS1@aol.com

dlynas22@aol.com

Programme Tutors/Coaches

Programme coaches are serving or former head teachers who have gained a national reputation for excellent school leadership and coaching skills and who are accredited assessors with the Scottish Qualification for Headship programme, upon which this programme is based.

Recognition

Readers who complete all aspects of the programme and who can demonstrate an improvement in their leadership skills to the satisfaction of their head teachers will be eligible for formal recognition of their project leadership skills by the General Teaching Council of Scotland. Details are available at their web site: www. gtcs.org.uk

Developing Excellent Team Leaders: Preliminary Thought Pieces

Introduction

The simple act of reading about leadership is not enough to guarantee development of leadership skills. But it is an important ingredient. The background readings, or thought pieces, in this programme are intended to provide handy access to the most up-to date thinking and findings about *school leadership*. Sometimes they take the form of short extracts from selected texts or the views of respected leaders and on other occasions they represent the thinking of an extensive range of experts on leadership, as distilled by the programme writers.

The first four thought pieces provided here are relevant to all of the workshop sessions in the programme *Developing Excellent Team Leaders*. It is recommended that they should be read first.

Thought Piece A provides a brief description of the *recurring* processes whereby a leader may build upon and develop existing leadership skills. The learning processes that are described in this thought piece underpin the structure of the entire programme.

Thought Piece B emphasises the fact that it is not possible to develop leadership skills merely by reading or by participating in courses that deal with leadership issues. One develops one's leadership skills by undertaking leadership roles, preferably with the assistance of a coach or mentor.

Thought Piece C emphasises the view that leadership in schools is not so much about the knowledge, skills and values of one individual but rather about *purposeful collaboration* among many individuals.

Thought Piece D explores further the particular contribution to leadership development that can be made by *peer coaching*.

The remaining thought pieces provide a mixture of general and specific information as a background to the leadership topics in focus in each workshop session and are included within relevant sessions.

Thought Piece A: How School Leaders Develop

The following steps are the key stages in a recurring process of how school leaders develop. The process is adapted from the research of *David Kolb* and *Richard Boyatzis* into experiential and self – directed learning, a form of learning that is particularly suited to those who hold a permanent or temporary leadership role.

Take action to deal with a (new) leadership challenge

If there is a difference in the way that school leaders learn, it is presumably because they are continually faced with actual leadership challenges and can therefore choose what they consider to be the ideal way of dealing with these experiences. They are then especially well-placed to select their own learning targets, identify relevant resources, decide on the learning methods that are most appropriate to their own needs and evaluate their own progress in ways that are at the very heart of *self-directed learning* (*Boyatzis,* 2002) Serving leaders have considerable scope to learn from the challenges they face – especially if they reflect upon them in a structured way.

Reflect On Action

Many personal leadership experiences may be fleeting and are unlikely to have any impact on personal learning, let alone pupil learning, unless leaders consciously reflect on what they did, how they went about it and why they acted as they did. Then they will be best placed to theorise about what might happen if things were done differently next time around. This is the message that is at the heart of *David Kolb's* ideas about the potential power of *experiential learning* (*Kolb* 1984) Reflection recurs throughout the experiential learning process and is of three kinds:

(a)   Self-evaluation

If you want to learn from any experience, the first step is to undertake some structured self-evaluation of your performance, assisted by such tools as quality indicators. What did you do? How did you go about things? Why did you do things in that way? (What was your thinking and where had this thinking come from?) What values were influencing your behaviour? What were the outcomes of your action? Could you have handled things better? These are the kinds of questions that you should seek answers to in an attempt to learn directly from any leadership experience.

Yet self-evaluation of personal experience is not enough in itself. The ways in which we assess an experience and its consequences and implications will clearly be influenced by the kind of people we are in terms of personal biases and in terms of the cultural contexts in which we find ourselves. Experience is not objective; it is neither person nor culture – free.

Self-evaluation of experience can easily slip into self-delusion, most often with people being too kind to themselves but sometimes with people being too hard on themselves. Self-evaluation, it would seem, is a necessary but insufficient condition of learning. It seems more likely that adult learning, like learning at any age, comes about through a *blend* of reflective processes

(b)   Observation and discussion

A great deal of learning can take place by being open to the views of others who have observed your personal practice and by observing how they do things. Peer group colleagues, senior colleagues, CPD officers and inspectors can all contribute to one's learning, providing one is willing to take their views on board and reflect upon them. The notion of *360º review* (See Workshop Session 6) whereby a person seeks and reflects upon the opinions of senior, junior and peer group colleagues is important here. And in recent times there has also been an increasing tendency for school leaders to invite pupils and parents to comment upon their practice.

It is especially useful, when reflecting upon personal experience, to consider the views of others who have had experiences similar to yours in similar contexts and who seem to have learned from them. Discussing and sharing similar experiences with other colleagues and listening to what they have to say about what they learned is a powerful means of personal development.

Such colleagues need not even be senior colleagues; there is much to be said for *peer coaching*, with colleagues sharing experiences, observing each other and helping each other to learn without feeling as if they are being judged. In this connection, anyone who has organised leadership workshops knows that participants consistently declare that the time they had to share experiences and views with their peers in an effort to make sense of those experiences and deal with them more effectively next time was extremely valuable – especially if those peers were facing similar challenges in similar contexts.

It is not surprising then that a major international survey of effective school systems in 2007 (*Barber and Mourshed*) discovered that strategies whereby teachers regularly observed each others' practice and shared knowledge of what works and what does not were some of the most effective of all ways of helping teachers and leaders to reflect upon and develop their skills. Such strategies also helped to shape a common aspiration and motivation among colleagues for improving the quality of instruction and hence pupil attainment. The topic of *peer coaching* is discussed in some detail in a later thought piece.

(c)   Reading

It is fashionable to dismiss 'theory', despite the observation of James C. Maxwell, one of Scotland's greatest ever scientists, that there is nothing more practical than a good theory. There is now an enormous body of research into school leadership, much of it based upon analysis by practitioners of what constitutes effective leadership and a lot of it is very good indeed.

When 'theory' is essentially a written account of the experiences and reflections of other leaders as they travelled a road that we are now travelling, then it is clear that people can learn vicariously from reading about such experiences in the same kind of way that they can learn vicariously through discussion with colleagues. No doubt some of these experiences will not be relevant to the particular contexts in which we find ourselves, but the competencies of the effective leader are generic enough to be relevant to many contexts. Instead of protesting that we do not have time for reading, perhaps we should consider the time we could save by reading about the leadership experiences of others and therefore having a better chance of getting things right first time around.

There is, of course, the simple fact that one should read for *information*. It is a poor leader who cannot find the time to keep up to date, for example, with the latest thinking about effective leadership, learning and teaching and the impact of national and local social trends on learning – not to mention national or local authority policies and procedures – before acting in ways that may well be less effective than they might otherwise have been.

In the last analysis any person will adopt a final view of her or his expertise based on self-evaluation. But by reflecting on the views of others, the self-evaluation will be more rigorous. Consequently that person will have a better chance of learning from experience and being able to theorise about the steps that should be taken in a given situation next time around.

Identify strengths and development needs in the approach

Undertaking the different kinds of reflection upon your leadership experiences will lead you to conclusions about how effective your leadership behaviour was in a given situation and to a consideration of the impact that your behaviour had in terms of improving things. Such reflection should, of course, be based on any available evidence, rather than assertion, assumption or mere speculation.

Reflection should focus particularly on the link between school leadership and pupil attainment so that the *processes* and the *products* of leadership can both be considered. You will want to know:

- What impact did my leadership have on the knowledge, skills and attitudes of my colleagues?
- What were the consequences for their approach to learning and teaching in the classroom?
- What were the consequences in turn for pupil performance?

Reflection of this kind will help you to discover where you fell short of achieving your purposes, in terms both of pupil performance and your own performance as a leader and to identify priorities for your personal development. As before, such conclusions are likely to be more rigorous, and therefore more valid, if you consider a *range* of perspectives and relevant evidence.

Identifying strengths and development needs in a valid and reliable way is the first step to identifying the means by which development needs might be addressed.

Draw up improvement plans and prepare a learning agenda for meeting needs

As an aspiring or serving leader, you and your pupils will both benefit if you draw up a two-part plan for improvement. One part of the plan will detail the steps you intend to take, working with and through your colleagues, to improve some aspect of stage, departmental or school provision. The other part of the plan will be more of a personal learning plan that details the steps you will take to improve upon your current leadership capacity. What kind of CPD do you need? What kind of resources do you need? What kinds of discussions with others do you need? What kind of reading may be of assistance to you? In brief, what are you going to do to improve your leadership behaviour in a way that will improve pupil learning?

Implement plans and learning agenda

Of its nature, this is likely to be the longest stage of the leadership development process, although everything depends on how extensive your improvement plans are. Having thought through and set down the steps you hope to take to achieve your objectives and having set yourself a due date for the 'completion' of a project that is intended to improve some aspect of pupil performance and your leadership skills, it is now time to set to work.

It may turn out that you have taken on too much in the first place. It may be that unforeseen circumstances necessitate adjustments and delays. So be prepared to adjust plans as you go along. There is nothing wrong in this. Planning and implementing are dynamically interlinked – as indeed are all stages of the improvement process, rather than being separate.

Do, however, maintain a steady focus on your original rationale for wanting to improve the given aspects of pupil and leadership performance in the first place. That way you will have a better chance of achieving your purposes, even if you have to adapt the means of achieving them as you go along.

Evaluate the impact on leadership development and on pupil learning

The cycle of learning is not complete – indeed it is a more like a continuing spiral rather than a cycle – until you have had an opportunity to evaluate in a rigorous way the impact of your improved leadership skills, directly or indirectly, on pupil performance, using your experiences in previous situations as a baseline from which to assess improvement in new situations.

Remarkably, thorough evaluation of progress is often neglected – if HMIE reports on schools are anything to go by.

If one hopes to develop as a leader, a series of questions have to be continually asked – and continually answered:

What new leadership knowledge have I gained?

- How has it improved my understanding of the concept of leadership?

- How have my leadership values changed?

- How have my leadership skills improved?

- What influence have I had on the values and skills of the teachers I lead?

- What have I done to help them improve their classroom performance?

- What has been the impact of all this on pupil attainment and achievement?

- What evidence do I have to support my answers to these questions?

This phase has links of course with the earlier stage in the process that involves identifying development needs.

NB: A useful range of tools to help you to answer these questions in a structured way and with a measure of objectivity now exists, including the range of quality indicators from *How Good Is Our School?*, 360º review documents such as the one provided in *Session 6* and the *Standard for Team Leadership* presented in the first workshop session.

Unsurprisingly, it becomes clear that leadership development that makes a difference depends upon an ongoing mixture of *practice* and *reflection upon practice,* with the developing leader asking her or himself the same kind of questions over and over again, being willing to consult a range of sources for possible answers and then using the answers to influence future practice.

References

Boyatzis, Richard, *Becoming A Resonant Leader* in Goleman, D. Boyatzis, R and McKee, A. *The New Leaders* (2002): London: Little Brown
Kolb, David A (1984) *Experiential Learning: Experience as the Source of Learning and Development.* Englewood Cliffs, NJ Prentice Hall

Thought Piece B: CPD and pupil attainment

Developing staff in ways that will have maximum impact on pupil attainment and achievement has been the focus of study over the last thirty years of two American researchers, Bruce Joyce and Beverley Showers – *see for example 'Student Achievement Through Staff Development (3rd ed)(2002): Alexandria VA*

For Joyce and Showers, effective Inset (CPD) originally involved up to *five* training components:

- The presentation of theory or awareness-raising of a new skill

- Demonstration or modelling of the new strategy or skill

- Initial practice of the skill in a protected or simulated setting

- Providing structured and open-ended feed-back about performance

- Coaching in the use of the new skill in an authentic setting

Each component contributed to a person's development but they had no doubt about which component contributed most to the kind of development that had the greatest impact on classroom practice and pupil attainment.

Follow-up research suggested that the first four CPD components resulted in only 25% of participants applying a new skill effectively in the classroom. However, when the fifth component - school-based mentored activity - was included as part of the development process, up to 95% of the participants transferred the skill into classroom practice.

In the last fifteen years Joyce and Showers have particularly emphasised the importance of *peer coaching* that avoids an evaluative or supervisory element. In their view, when teachers observe each other, it is the *teacher* who is the coach and the *observer* who is coached. They are now much less sure of the value of feedback that is judgemental in nature. They found over years of research that such feedback may destroy rather than promote collaborative activity. Accordingly, in the context of peer coaching, as opposed say to a case of performance monitoring, it is better to think of feedback as being informed professional dialogue among the participants involved.

In essence, the observing teacher is providing the observed teacher with information that he or she would not otherwise have had. It is then up to the observed teacher to add this information to his or her own self-evaluation so that the observed teacher can make more informed choices about what to do next further to improve his or her teaching skills.

Reference has already been made to a major inter-national survey by *Michael Barber* and *Mona Mourshed* (2007) which confirmed not only that developing teacher skills was a major, if unsurprising, contributor to school improvement but that peer coaching was the most effective strategy for developing these skills.

The research related to improving learning and teaching skills in the classroom but it seems likely that peer coaching is equally relevant to improving leadership and management skills. (See further later)

So far as feedback is concerned, the writers of this programme take a middle view. They readily accept that the most useful form of feedback, as with any form of evaluation, is self-observation. But they maintain, as noted elsewhere, that the best self-observation will include consideration of the observations of others – literally and metaphorically.

Feedback that has an evaluatory element has its place so long as the evaluator is sensitive to the needs of the learner in an atmosphere of mutual trust. A mentor or coach must also be wise enough to accept that, in the last analysis, learners must be allowed to decline advice and adopt their own approach, providing of course that any approach they adopt is within a core of agreed policies.

Thought Piece C: Distributed Leadership in Schools

'There is an increasing weight of empirical evidence that demonstrates the potential and potency of teacher leadership. The old order of leadership equalling headship is unlikely to prevail. The new order is premised upon a view of leadership that is distributed and empowers those closest to the classroom to undertake leadership tasks and actions. Leadership is then not about the knowledge, skills and values of one individual but rather about *purposeful collaboration* among many individuals. In the last analysis, head teachers still have to take final decisions, as being formally accountable to the local authority. But in many ways the distinctions between followers and leaders will begin to blur. This opens up the possibility for all teaching staff to become leaders at various times and to be the creators of change, not merely the recipients.'

Adapted from Alma Harris, Daniel Muijs (2004) *Improving Schools Through Teacher Leadership:* Open University Press

Thought Piece D: Peer Coaching

Reference has been made in both previous thought pieces to the power of peer coaching. Peer coaching is a particular form of *collaborative* CPD and over the years a number of studies across the world have indicated that collaborative CPD has had a positive impact on classroom learning and teaching in terms of:

- improving the repertoire of learning and teaching strategies that teachers have

- the ability of teachers to match their repertoire of skills to the specific needs of their pupils

- the self-esteem and confidence of teachers

- the commitment of teachers to development of their skills

- improvement in pupil learning

Peer coaching involves teachers working together on a sustained basis to plan programmes of study, lesson planning, lesson delivery and lesson analysis and is based essentially on observation and mutual support.

Such coaching may involve working with peers, senior colleagues or junior colleagues in the same school or department or across departments and even across schools. Or it may involve working with LEA, HEI or other professional colleagues. No matter. The key point is, as the title of peer coaching implies, that what is involved is a *mutual* and *reciprocal* approach in which all the participants have the opportunity to observe and be observed and to take part in professional dialogue about what worked or did not work, no matter the posts or relative status of the participants.

Defined thus, peer coaching is not quite the same as mentoring with its connotations of a wise and experienced practitioner advising a junior or inexperienced colleague. Mentoring may, of course, be linked with peer coaching in those cases where coaches agree that they need the advice of a more experienced colleague.

As Joyce and Showers have suggested (see earlier) peer coaching should be non-judgemental and non –threatening. It is concerned with a school's development agenda rather than its accountability agenda. In this connection, the focus of observation and dialogue should be decided by the teacher being observed. Peer coaching is based on a form of informed self-evaluation so it is up to the observed teacher to make use of insights to improve teaching performance.

Unsurprisingly, the process works best in an atmosphere of mutual trust and respect or at the very least in situations where participants agree to be involved and are comfortable about working with one another. It is also likely to involve some careful timetabling so that participants can have agreed times for joint planning, joint observation and joint dialogue about outcomes and next steps.

The findings about the value of peer coaching as described above relate to improving classroom learning and teaching but there is no reason why the same approach, based upon the same principles, should not also apply to leadership and management development. Thus there would be considerable value in aspiring and serving leaders working together and learning from each other in an effort to develop their leadership skills. The activities that comprise peer coaching reflect many of the points that are made about leadership development in the model described in *Thought Piece A.*

A peer coaching process for school leaders, as with classroom teachers, would involve a *planning* dimension, an *observation* dimension and a *reflective* dimension. Thus, for example, a couple of team leaders might discuss how they work with colleagues to formulate, implement and evaluate school or departmental policies. They might jointly plan the agendas for meetings that they lead, observe each other's leadership of their respective meetings and discuss afterwards how successful the meetings were. In another example, two team leaders might agree to shadow each other for a given period of time and for a given purpose. Initiatives like this would require careful organisation and some time support but could be well worth the effort.

We return to the notion of peer coaching when we discuss *learning rounds* in Session 6

This concludes the thought pieces that are relevant to all workshop sessions.

Workshop Session 1: A Standard for Team Leadership

Workshop Session 1: A Standard for Team Leader-ship

Introduction

In 1982, HMI issued an analysis of the functions of school managers in Scotland's secondary schools at head, depute head, assistant head and departmental head levels. They found that middle managers such as departmental heads devoted their 'responsibility time' largely to administrative functions such as ordering materials, issuing timetables and syllabuses and allocating accommodation. There was little evidence of departmental heads taking responsibility for monitoring the quality of learning, teaching and pupil behaviour beyond their own classrooms, of reviewing the performance of and encouraging the development of their colleagues or of promoting a team approach. Departmental colleagues were largely left to get on with things in their own way.

When the former Strathclyde Region issued in 1986 a document entitled *Managing Progress* there was something of an outcry among departmental heads who objected to the suggestion that they should have a line management responsibility for such matters. 'I see they are trying to turn us into managers', was the complaint of one disgruntled departmental head.

Fast forward some twenty years to a conference of middle managers in England who identified the follow-ing key issues and changing roles for that level of management:

Key Issues for Team Leaders*

- A focus on learning and teaching – not simply routine administration
- The importance of monitoring and evaluating the work of colleagues
- The need for CPD in Team leadership

Changing Roles for Team Leaders

- The learning heart of the school

- A key component of the school's intellectual capacity
- Knowledge managers, facilitating the work of teams
- Leaders of multi-disciplinary teams
- A recognisable team of leaders with a clear collec-tive vision to improve learning and teaching

A recent survey of depute heads in England highlighted similar concerns. Overall it was clear that managers at departmental and senior management levels were keen to get away from the idea that they were merely administrative functionaries. From their point of view, leadership at these levels should ultimately be about improving learning and teaching - and consequently attainment – as it is at headship level.

At the same time, both middle and aspiring senior managers recognised the importance of being supported by relevant CPD if they were to be equipped to meet the challenges of these enhanced roles.

Learning Outcomes

By the end of this first workshop session readers will have:

- ✓ Read a number of thought pieces related to the functions and qualities of school leaders at middle and senior level
- ✓ Re-clarified their ideas about the nature of leader-ship and management at these levels
- ✓ Evaluated their current abilities in terms of a *Standard for Team Leadership*
- ✓ Reflected on the link between leadership and learning

Workshop Activities: Introduction

The purpose of each workshop is to involve the reader in:

- reading thought pieces related to a given leader-ship issue

- reflection on personal experience of that issue

- discussions with colleagues where possible about their experiences of, and insights into, the same issue

- reflection on feedback from other groups and the wider world of research about the same issue

Some activities and related feedback are common to both aspiring middle managers such as heads of department and to aspiring senior managers. In other cases, readers are invited to undertake the activities and the associated feedback that relate most to their needs.

There are four activities related to *Workshop Session 1*. Please begin by reading the thought pieces that are supplied below. They all relate to the role and functions of leaders at different levels and to the qualities that are the mark of an effective leader.

We begin by exploring the distinctions between teaching and leading and between leading and managing at different levels.

We then consider the distinction in meaning and signif-icance of key concepts such as leadership, management and administration.

Readers are then introduced to a *Standard for Team Leadership* and are invited to evaluate their current levels of experience in terms of that Standard.

A final activity explores by means of a case study approach how aspects of leadership, or lack of leadership, can have an impact on what happens in the classroom and invites readers to consider what they would have done, and what should have been done, in a given situation. Reflections on the activities should be shared with colleagues, if possible.

*The term 'team leader' is taken throughout this text to refer to two categories of leader.

- Those who aspire to a middle management post such as head of department, pastoral leader or coordinator of learning support or cross-curricular themes

- Serving middle managers who aspire to a senior management post in a school.

Workshop Session1: A Standard for Team Leadership:

Thought Piece 1.1: The Role of HT, DHT, PT and Teacher:

In Scotland, all teachers share the same basic duties as follows:

- Teaching assigned classes together with associated preparation and correction

- Assessing, recording and reporting on the work of pupils

- Preparing pupils for examinations and assisting in their administration

But their other grade-related duties also have much in common, as the following table of teachers' duties in Scotland shows.

Head Teacher (DHT)	Principal Teacher	Teacher
Responsibility for the leadership, good management and strategic direction of the school	Responsibility for the leader-ship, good management and strategic direction of colleagues	Participating in issues related to school planning, and raising achievement
To manage the health and safety of all within the school premises	Implementation of school policies dealing with guidance issues, pastoral care, assess-ment and pupil welfare	Promoting and safeguarding the health, welfare and safety of pupils
Responsibility for school policy for the behaviour management of pupil	Contributing to the develop-ment of school policy in relation to the behaviour management of pupils	Contributing towards good order and the wider needs of the school
The management of all staff, and the provision of professional advice and guidance to colleagues	The management and guidance of colleagues	Providing advice and guidance to pupils on issues related to their education
The management and development of the school curriculum	Curriculum development and quality assurance	Developing the school curriculum
To act as adviser to the Parent Council and to participate in the selection and appointment of staff in the school	(To participate in the selection and appointment of staff to the school if invited)	

To promote continuing professional development of all staff and to ensure that all staff have an annual review of their development needs	Reviewing the CPD needs, career development and per-formance of colleagues	Undertaking appropriate and agreed continuing professional development
Working in partnership with parents, other professionals, agencies and schools	Working in partnership with colleagues, parents, other specialist agencies and staff in other schools as appropriate	Working in partnership with parents, support staff and other professionals

Given also the close relationship between leadership skills and teaching skills, it is obvious that a collegiate style of working is essential in Scotland's schools if pupil achievement and attainment is to be raised.

Thought Piece: 1.2: Organisational Purposes

We may think of a school as an organisation that has two essential purposes. On the one hand the school and its staff have a fundamental role to play in meeting the learning needs and expectations of the pupils who attend it, and their parents. On the other hand, those same members of staff have personal needs that must be met if they are to be best equipped to meet the needs of others.

The challenge for any school leader at any level is to engage in the kind of leadership behaviour that will find a proper balance between these sometimes competing sets of needs. There are attainment targets for pupils to achieve and tasks to be undertaken; there are also staff and their needs to be taken into consideration. The one will never be fully achieved without the other. But the first might well be achieved *through* the latter.

Thought Piece 1.3: Leadership Functions and Qualities

(a)   What do excellent team leaders do?
(b)   What are excellent team leaders like?

Actually there is no simple answer to either of these fundamental questions and certainly there is no one-size-fits-all model of team leadership that is guaranteed to work all the time and everywhere. But extensive research into team leadership allows us to make some assertions with reasonable confidence.

(a)   What do excellent school leaders do?

The central task of school leaders at any level is to improve pupil achievement and attainment. All the evidence indicates that such improvement in pupil performance depends upon improvement in the quality of learning and teaching in the classroom. It cannot be mandated from outside.

So the role of team leaders is to work with and through their teaching colleagues to improve teaching performance and hence pupil performance within their given area of responsibility. It is as simple (or as complex) as that, as leadership guru Michael Fullan might say.

Teacher performance is in itself a function of five re-lated factors:

- The knowledge and understanding of teachers

- The teaching skills of teachers
- The beliefs and values of teachers
- The context in which teachers work
- Levels of teacher motivation

Leaders contribute to improving these aspects of teacher performance through their professional practice in terms of 12 sets of functions:

✓ Building and sharing a vision
✓ Agreeing plans, policies, aims and objectives
✓ Clarifying roles, systems and procedures
✓ Fostering a collegiate and collaborative approach to meeting needs
✓ Motivating and inspiring
✓ Consulting, negotiating and deciding
✓ Delegating and distributing leadership functions
✓ Developing, supporting and providing resources
✓ Managing conflict
✓ Networking with parents and the wider community
✓ Monitoring and evaluating
✓ Recognising and rewarding

(b)   What are excellent team leaders like?

Every effective team leader has relevant knowledge and understanding, a repertoire of core skills and a set of core values.

Values come first. Team leadership is a moral enterprise that the best leaders see in terms of service to the needs of children. Thus they model the following:

- a due respect for themselves and for others
- integrity and a commitment to ethical practices
- a commitment to the education of the whole child and to every child
- a commitment to equality of opportunity, in-clusiveness and to the values of a democratic society
- a committed to lifelong learning, including their own

Associated with their values, effective team leaders demonstrate certain key *personal attributes.* These include:

- open-mindedness and in particular a willingness to learn from others
- flexibility in their thinking, within their system of core values as described above
- passion in the pursuit of those same values
- perseverance and optimism in the face of ad-versity

As well as the personal attributes described above, successful team leaders use a range of *interpersonal skills* that may be grouped together under what has become known as *'emotional intelligence'* – the ability to understand and manage one's own feelings and the ability to understand and help others to manage their feelings.

Emotional intelligence is essential as team leaders seek:

- to inspire and motivate their colleagues
- to communicate with and to listen effectively to colleagues
- to understand and manage the micro-politics of a situation
- to identify and develop individual talent
- to harness the range of available talents in a team approach

Team leaders also demonstrate a range of *intellectual* skills, including:

- the ability to develop overall strategies, plans, policies and procedures for school improvement
- decision-making and decision-taking skills
- the ability to use data to evaluate the impact of school provision on pupil outcomes.

Finally effective team leaders make sure that they are up to date in their *knowledge and understanding* of four key areas of activity:

- Teaching for effective learning
- Contemporary developments in education policy at national, local and school level
- Contemporary developments in society and their impact on learning and teaching
- The principles and practice of leadership and in particular the management of change

These qualities relate to three permeating elements that underpin the professional practice of school leaders as described in the *Standard for Team Leaders (See later)*

- Strategic vision, values and aims

- Knowledge and understanding

- Personal qualities and interpersonal skills

Thought Piece 1.4: Excellent teachers and excellent leaders of teachers

'The leadership role – as opposed to the teaching role – is to be the 'glue' in the organisation, not it is hoped in the sense of 'gumming up' the works – though those whom you manage will inevitably see it that way at times – but in the sense of holding the organisation together.

The first post in which a teacher has to plan, organise, direct and control the work of other colleagues involves a fundamental change in the criteria for job success. Many learn the lesson the hard way.

Throughout the educational process, success as a student teacher tends to depend on demonstrating and exploiting one's own ideas and talents. This is also the focus in one's first teaching appointment. As a leader, on the other hand, success depends on using the ideas and talents of a team, on arriving at decisions and actions to which team members feel committed and on ensuring that that they are put into effect. Though you may not feel that someone else's idea is quite as good as your own, you may be wise to back that idea, particularly if the person who puts it forward has a key role in implementation.

Thus the leader is less concerned with *being* a resource than with *using* resources, not that leadership by example is unimportant. Team leaders often fulfil both classroom and leadership roles, and the danger is that one forgets that behaviour which succeeds in the classroom may be different from that required to motivate the team.'

(Adapted from Everard, Morris and Wilson (2004), pp 4,5)

Thought Piece 1.5: Leadership and management

Whilst leadership and management skills are complementary and closely linked, it is important to distinguish between them clearly. In everyday language, it is common to talk about 'providing a lead'. However, we often recognise that someone can be an effective operational manager or administrator whilst not necessarily being an effective leader. Here it may be more common to refer to someone 'managing on a day-to-day basis', 'managing the budget' or 'managing resources'. We tend not to use 'leading' in these instances. Leadership, therefore, is closely related to strategic management but distinguishable from operational and administrative management tasks in a number of respects:

Leadership is about setting out and inspiring others with a longer-term strategic vision for the future; without such leadership, management tends to have a narrow and restrictive focus on the day-to-day.

Leadership is about challenging and changing some of the key priorities; without such leadership, management tends to focus more on the best use of available resources to meet a specific priority.

Leadership is about setting and reviewing objectives in relation to a clear strategic view of what is to be achieved; without such leadership, management may focus mainly on setting up systems to take forward particular objectives without questioning their appropriateness.

Leadership involves winning hearts and minds and inspiring others to want to perform consistently to the highest standards; without such leadership, management may be more concerned with setting out and monitoring operational guidelines which restrict innovation and creativity rather than empowering staff to perform.

Leadership involves looking beyond the school and working with others who can contribute to school improvement; without such leadership, management may tend to evaluate success against a limited and inward-looking view of what is possible.

Leadership sets out and builds an over-arching school ethos of achievement and success; without such leadership, management may focus only on means of monitoring and tracking performance, without promoting improvement.

(Improving Leadership in Scottish Schools, HMIE 2000)

Thought Piece 1.6: Leadership, Management, Administration
The concepts of leadership and management over-lap with each other and with the related notion of administration. Indeed there are considerable variations in meaning between the terms depending upon where you are in the world. In the USA, for example, 'administration' relates to concepts of national government

11

whereas in Britain the same term usually relates to notions of clerical activity.

For the purposes of this programme, we suggest the following:

- Leadership is particularly concerned with shaping and sharing with colleagues a vision of a desired future for the safety and educational well-being of pupils
- Management is concerned with the efficient and effective maintenance of current organi-sational arrangements and with the day-to-day implementation of the plans, policies and procedures by which a vision may be achieved
- Administration is concerned with the effective recording and maintenance of documentation related to the processes of leadership and management

Team leaders frequently experience tensions between the competing demands of leadership, management, administration and their own teaching duties. They can find it difficult to decide the balance of time between higher order functions designed to improve staff, pupil and school performance (leadership), routine maintenance of present operations (management) and paperwork (administration). All three have their place but it would be a matter for considerable concern if the professional activities of a team leader were largely taken up with administrative functions to the exclusion of any leadership functions.

This completes the thought pieces for this workshop session but see also the bibliography.

Session 1: Workshop Activities

Activity WS 1.1: Key Distinctions (Aspiring to middle management)

Individually, note down your responses to the following:

What for you is the key difference, if any, between being an excellent *teacher* and being an excellent *leader* of teachers?

In particular, what would you say are the key skills that you would need as a leader that you might not need as a teacher? Reflect for about 10 minutes on this. Your reading of the *Thought Pieces 1.3 and 1.4 in particular* should help your reflections.

Share your personal responses with colleagues if possible.

Activity WS: 1.1: Role differences (Aspiring to senior management)

Individually, reflect on and note down your responses to the following:

(a)   What are the main challenges for you in undertaking the leadership functions of a *senior* manager compared to the leadership functions of a *middle* manager?

(b)   What is the difference, if any, in the *(i) knowledge (ii) skills and (iii) values* that are looked for in a senior manager as opposed to a middle manager? List your responses under those three headings.

You may find that the *Thought Pieces* will assist your reflections.

Activity WS1.2: Leader or manager? (Aspiring to middle management)

The distinction between leadership and management has been described in a number of ways, as exemplified by *Thought Piece 1.5*. Have a read at that thought piece and then:

(a) Jot down below any six *activities* that you associate with 'leading'. Now jot down any six *activities* that you associate with 'managing.' You are offered one of each to start with. Focus on action words rather than descriptive words. Spend about 5 minutes on this. Then share your ideas with colleagues if possible.

Leading: (a) Visioning   (b)   (c)   (d)   etc

Managing: (a) Planning (b)   (c)   (d)   etc

(b) **Table A** below offers a range of statements about leadership and management that are adapted from *Thought Piece 1.5.*

Mark a cross in one of the columns 1-5 in the table to indicate where on the continuum between each set of statements your current priorities lie. The activity should take no more than 5 minutes. Later you will be invited to examine your responses so that you can identify any changes you may wish to make to improve as a leader and manager.

Table A: Leader or Manager? (Aspiring to middle management)

	1	2	3	4	5	
I am concerned with focusing on the day-to-day demands of my duties	.	.	.	.	.	I am concerned with setting out and inspiring others with a longer-term strategic vision for the future
I am concerned with focusing on the best use of available resources to meet a specific priority	.	.	.	.	.	I am concerned with challenging and changing some of the key priorities
I am concerned with focusing mainly on following systems and policies to take forward particular objectives	.	.	.	.	.	I am concerned with setting and reviewing objectives in relation to a clear strategic view of what is to be achieved
I am concerned with setting out and monitoring the implementation of operational guidelines	.	.	.	.	.	I am concerned with winning hearts and minds and inspiring others to want to perform consistently to the highest standards
I am concerned with evaluating success in terms of an inward-looking view of what is possible.	.	.	.	.	.	I am concerned with looking beyond the school and working with others who can contribute to school improvement

	1	2	3	4	5	
I am concerned with evaluating success in terms of an inward-looking view of what is possible.	.	.	.	.	.	I am concerned with looking beyond the school and working with others who can contribute to school improvement
I am concerned with maintaining positive behaviour in my classes	.	.	.	.	.	I am concerned to set out and build an over-arching school ethos of achievement and success

Activity WS 1.2: Management, administration, leadership, teaching

(Aspiring to senior management)

Read again *Thought Pieces 1.5 and 1.6* which discuss the relationships and the differences between leadership, management and administration.

Read the remit of a DHT and the week's log of activities of that DHT which follows. As you read each activity, allocate to it a Remit Number from the remit that is supplied and then use the initial **M, A, L, T** to indicate whether you think the activity calls *mainly* for management, administrative, leadership or teaching skills.

What general conclusions do you come to about the distribution of activities of this DHT in the week in question and his/her *potential* contribution as a leader to school improvement and raised pupil attainment and achievement? Spend around 15 – 20 minutes on this activity and discuss it with colleagues if possible.

A Week in the Life of a DHT

A summary of the major activities undertaken by a DHT in one week is provided in the following pages.

The remit of the DHT includes eight broad areas:

1. To contribute proposals to the overall vision, strategy, planning and evaluation of the school's progress
2. To provide a management overview of all provision for S5/S6 students
3. To manage the implementation of the school's CPD and PSE policies
4. To provide an SMT link with:

    4(a) certain subject departments

    4(b) the school's support staff

    4(c) the School Pupil Council

5. To act as regent for Newly Qualified Teachers
6. To contribute to the general supervision of all pupil behaviour
7. To teach assigned classes as required
8. To write up and maintain documentation relating to all of the above

Monday 26 November

7.10: Arrived in office .Checked emails. Discussion with janitor about lay out of seating in assembly hall for Chaplain/S1 Assembly regarding Christmas parcels

7.50: Discussion, arising from DM minutes, with link PT subject regarding ongoing difficulties with a member of dept struggling with pupil behaviour problems

8.15: Short meeting with a teacher who has agreed to allow another colleague to observe him teaching a difficult class

8.25: Welcome meeting with newly appointed senior technician and took a few minutes to introduce him to other colleagues

8.35: Met with two S6 girls to discuss travel arrangements for a Primary School Dance Group which they have entered into a competition as part of primary-secondary liaison

8.50: S1 Assembly with chaplain to promote Christmas parcels and Carol Services

9.10: Cuppa with chaplain

9.35: Checked over a UCAS personal statement, in advance of an interview with applicant

9.45: Met with a parent and S5 pupil to discuss possible change of teaching arrangements prior to their meeting with a psychiatrist

10.15: Meeting with Admin and Finance Officer to prepare information on school spending to share with the Student Council

10.30: Met with an S5 pupil, whose PT Guidance is absent, to discuss his request to change subject.

10.40: Phone call with Quality Improvement Manager about a possible place on an international visit for a member of staff

10.50: Interval. Playground duty and chatting to pupils

11.05: Phone call with mother of an S6 pupil, victim of a serious assault in the community, just returned to school, to update one another on events in the interim

11.15: Monthly Link Meeting with Librarian to discuss current issues

12.00: Congratulated PTG on her S6 Enterprise team's performance at a science festival

12.10: Visit to HE department as SMT link to see completed meals prepared by S4 Int 2 pupils for their Hospitality prelim

12.30: Early lunch with SMT colleagues. (Always a working lunch) Awaited 3 S2 pupils detained for earlier misbehaviour. Accompanied them to cafeteria where I was covering for absent DHT.

13.30: Caught up on things to do

14.00: Worked on a schedule of meetings to allow me to meet with each link department following a recent school review

14.20: Discussion with Head Girl about the Senior Disco she has organised for Friday evening

14.40: Meeting with NQTs as part of their mentoring support programme. Topic: The Role of the Parent Council

15.10: Meeting with subject PT re possible involvement in study visit abroad as part of CPD

15.30: Bus supervision rota

16.00: Thinking time, filing time and then off home at 16.45

Tuesday 27 November

7.10: Arrived in office .Checked emails. Read over first draft of School Handbook ahead of SMT meeting. Read over minutes of link departmental meetings from previous week. Prepared notes for meeting with SCA. Read over two UCAS applications.

8.30: Meeting with SCA for assistance with today's tasks

8.45: S2 Assembly with chaplain re Christmas parcels and carol service

9.55: Meeting with pastoral team to plan next term's phase pf the PSE programme

10.50: Interval and playground duty

11.05: Meeting with community police officer to discuss her role with a view to possible changes in arrangements

12.00: SMT meeting – discussion about timetable, staffing and curriculum for next session

12.45: Lunch with SMT

1.05: Supervision in cafeteria and playground

1.35: Meeting of the Student Council, chaired by S2 pupil

2.30: Weekly cover period in the time out room

3.30: Weekly meeting with the HT and EIS rep to discuss agenda for next meeting

3.45: Attendance at Technical Department meeting on assessment issues

4.25: Consolidated the day's events. Read over two UCAS submissions

4.50 Sent email to DHT in another school enquiring about his 33 period week arrangements ahead of next SMT meeting

5.00: Left for home

Wednesday 28 November

8.10: Meeting with SCA to discuss tasks for today

8.35: Front door monitoring

8.45: S3 Assembly to promote preparation of Christmas parcels for the elderly

9.00: Meeting with teacher in link department and union rep re pupil behaviour management. Explored issues of competence and agreed arrangements for CPD for the teacher in question

9.30: Helped pupil with UCAS application form

9.50: Weekly meeting of SMT to discuss CfE progress in each department

10.50: Interval. Supervision in junior cafeteria

11.10: Catching up with admin

11.40: Interview with parent and pupil re abuse. Matter to be referred to social services

12.10: Observation of NQT to discuss with PT any CPD needs

2.10: Checked Authority website for forthcoming CPD opportunities. Prepared CPD notes for inclusion in monthly staff bulletin

2.30: Observation of a second NQT for discussion with PT on CPD needs

3.30: Wrote up notes on both observations of NQTs

4.00: Drafted a survey for parents, pupils and staff on Study Leave Arrangements

4.30: Thinking time about the day and notes of things to do

5.00: Left for home

Thursday 29 November

7.10: Dealt with emails

8.00: Dealt with online CPD course requests from a few members of staff

8.40: Daily meeting with SCA to discuss today's requirements

8.45: S4 Assembly re Christmas parcels followed by coffee with school chaplain

9.40: UCAS interviews with two applicants

10.00: Dropped into one or two classes of link department teachers to chat briefly about any support concerns

11.10: Assembly with S6 on Christmas parcels followed by some admin

12.30: Lunch with SMT followed by supervision in junior cafeteria

12.55: Meeting with member of staff regarding a parental complaint. Complaint unwarranted after earlier investigation and teacher assured of support of HT/ SMT

2.30: Attendance at Maths DM on new materials/methods for new S1 programme of studies

3.40: Read through next batch of UCAS submissions in advance of meeting with applicants

4.10: Caught up with telephone messages left by various colleagues during the day

4.30: Checked over to-do list

4.45: Second glance at DHT application forms in advance of a leeting meeting with HT colleague from another school tomorrow

5.45: Left for home

Friday 30th November

7.15: Checked emails followed by some admin

8.00: Meeting with librarian in her GLOW mentor role to discuss training issues for staff and pupils

8.20: Welcomed back a link PT from long term absence

8.35: Meeting with SCA to discuss day's activities

8.50: S5 Assembly on Christmas parcels

9.15: Meeting with acting PT regarding arrangements when absent PT's phased return commences. Thanked acting PT and praised her contribution

9.30: Leeting meeting to assist HT colleague to leet two DHT posts

11.30: Meeting with PTG to brief me on update of Student Council activities

11.50: Meeting with student teacher to discuss his end of placement report

12.10: Lunch with SMT

12.30: Jotted down some thoughts for afternoon SMT meeting

12.45: SMT meeting to continue timetabling, staffing and curriculum issues for next session and revision of school handbook. Brief discussion of 33-period week. More discussion required

1.50: Signed mail and dealt with other admin

3.00: Chatted over coffee with HT about Senior Disco and weekend ahead, followed by bus supervision

3.45: Left for home – attended senior disco from 8 until midnight. Danced six times!

A Standard for Team Leadership

Introduction

A Standard for Team Leadership sets out the core purpose and desired outcomes of team leadership in schools and describes the professional actions and key elements of expertise that are expected of team leaders at different levels. The Standard serves to inform, challenge and inspire aspiring and serving middle and senior managers and offers a model against which they can match their current levels of experience in order to determine their strengths and areas for development.

The Standard has been derived from the *Standard for Headship* in Scotland's Schools and although it does not have a formal status it provides a useful tool for thinking about development needs. It has also been used as a guide for preparing this training and development programme for aspiring and serving middle and senior managers.

The Core Purpose and Desired Outcomes of Team Leadership:

Team leaders take the professional actions, permeated by key elements of expertise that will create the kind of learning organisation that will help pupils to become successful learners, confident individuals, responsible citizens and effective contributors

Professional Actions:

The professional actions of a team leader are grouped under five areas of activity:

- Leading and Managing Learning and Teaching

- Leading and Developing People

- Leading Change and Improvement

- Managing Resources

- Building Community

Key Elements of Expertise:

The key elements of expertise that underpin and per-meate the professional actions of a team leader are:

- Professional Values and Personal Commitments

- Professional Skills and Abilities

- Professional Knowledge and Understanding

Illustrations of these elements are provided in lists that follow later.

Note: Although listed separately, the essential elements and the areas of activity are interdependent within each other and dynamically linked across each other. Thus one's values are likely to be influenced by one's knowledge and understanding and are likely in their turn to influence one's priorities for action and the way in which one carries action out.

Similarly, the benefits of a commitment to relevant values, together with a commitment to develop relevant knowledge and skills, are restricted unless they lead to effective professional activity within the five areas described.

And finally, the five areas of activity are themselves interconnected. Thus, leading and managing learning and teaching is achieved through leading and developing people and leading change and improvement cannot be achieved without appropriate management of resources.

The lists that follow provide illustrations of the kinds of activity that are most commonly undertaken by middle managers and senior managers. The first step in the leadership learning process is to assess current levels of experience and ability to carry out these activities. This will help learners to plan how to build on their current levels of experience and expertise.

Activity WS1.3: Standard for Team Leadership: Self-evaluation Aspiring to Middle Management: Individually, use the sample illustrations of essential activities listed below to assess your current levels of experience in the functions that are listed. You will be invited to return to the results later when you are called upon to prepare a personal learning plan for developing your leadership skills.

Standard for Team Leadership (aspiring to middle management)

Illustrations

The lists below provide illustrations of the professional actions that are expected of an aspiring *middle manager*. They are not exhaustive, nor are they appropriate to all middle managers in all situations. Assign a code rating to your levels of experience in each of the listed activities, using the following scale:

6 (extensive experience)

5 (considerable experience)

 4 (good experience)

3 (satisfactory experience)

2 (little experience)

1 (no experience)

NB: It is recognised that some aspiring middle managers will have had little or no experience of some of these functions and activities. All the more reason for them to identify what their priority learning needs are.

List 1: The Professional Actions of Middle Managers

Leading and Managing Learning and Teaching: Within a given remit, a middle manager:

- ✓ Communicates a clear vision of the team's role in enhancing pupil attainment and achievement

- ✓ Develops and agrees policies, methods and materials for effective learning, teaching and assessment

- ✓ Sets high standards of behaviour and attendance and a culture of challenge and support to enable children and young people to engage with their own learning

- ✓ Evaluates and reviews classroom practice and exper-ience

Leading and Developing People: Within a given remit, a middle manager:

- ✓ Develops effective strategies for staff induction, profess-ional review and ongoing CPD, including coaching and mentoring

- ✓ Shares leadership with colleagues by agreeing and delegating individual and team roles and accountabilities

- ✓ Supports colleagues to achieve high standards of performance and takes appropriate action when performance is unsatisfactory

- ✓ Creates, maintains and enhances a collegiate style of working within the team and alliances between the team and other colleagues

Leading Change and Improvement: Within a given remit, a middle manager:

- ✓ Audits existing policies, plans and procedures at least annually and identifies improvement priorities

- ✓ Draws up action plans, in conjunction with colleagues, to address priorities for improvement in provision

- ✓ Implements plans and monitors progress towards embedding new approaches

- ✓ Evaluates the impact of new approaches on practice and pupil attainment and achievement

Managing Resources: Within a given remit, a middle manager:

- ✓ Negotiates resources and finance and allocates them at team and individual level to support departmental maintenance and improvement plans and policies for learning, teaching and assessment

- ✓ Ensures that team resources and facilities meet depart-mental health and safety requirements

- ✓ Controls spending within agreed budgets and evaluates its impact on learning and teaching in terms of cost-effectiveness within the department

Building Community: Within a given remit, a middle manager:

- ✓ Works closely with parents to encourage learning, teaching and attainment

- ✓ Builds links with the authority and other schools and agencies that support learning

- ✓ Promotes policies and practices that encourage inclusive-ness and a culture of respect for all

Activity WS1.3 (aspiring to middle management) continued

In *Lists 2- 4* which follow, use the following HMIE rating scale to indicate your current levels of expertise in the various attributes that are listed:

6 (excellent)

5 (very good)

4 (good)

3 (satisfactory)

2 (weak)

1 (unsatisfactory)

List 2: Professional Values and Personal Commitments: Within a given remit, a middle manager:

- ✓ Articulates a clear vision and ensures that it is shared and understood among colleagues

- ✓ Is committed to integrity and ethical practice with regard to equality, social justice and inclusion

- ✓ Is committed to and encourages due respect for self and others in and across departments

- ✓ Is committed to critical self-evaluation and ongoing professional development and encourages and supports it in colleagues

List 3: Knowledge and Understanding: Within a given remit, a middle manager knows and understands:

- ✓ The principles of effective learning and teaching, including the use of new technologies, and how to manage these

- ✓ Local and national priorities and the roles and structures of relevant bodies and their implications for colleagues

- ✓ Strategies for raising attainment and achieving excellence

- ✓ The principles and practice of team leadership

- ✓ The principles of leading change and policy development and implementation

- ✓ Social trends as they impact on plans, policies, aims and methods

- ✓ Self-evaluation and improvement strategies, quality assur-ance systems and the tools that support an evidence-based approach to decision-making

List 4: Personal Qualities and Interpersonal Skills: Within a given remit, a middle manager:

- ✓ Understands and can control personal emotions

- ✓ Understands and can help others control their emotions

- ✓ Creates and maintains a positive atmosphere and team spirit

- ✓ Takes account of the values and views of others, including children and young people

- ✓ Inspires and motivates others

- ✓ Thinks strategically

- ✓ Uses effective decision-making processes and problem-solving techniques

- ✓ Communicates effectively in terms both of providing information and inviting and listening to feedback

- ✓ Shows political insight related to issues of power and influence and a variety of agendas

Activity WS1.3: Self-evaluation for aspiring senior managers

Illustrations

List 1 below provides illustrations of the professional actions that are expected of a satisfactory *senior manager*. Evaluate your levels of experience of each activity to date, using the following scale:

6 (extensive experience)

5 (considerable experience)

4 (good experience)

3 (satisfactory experience)

2 (little experience)

1 (no experience)

List 1: The Professional Actions of Senior Managers

Leading and Managing Learning and Teaching: Within a given remit, a senior manager:

- ✓ Communicates a clear vision of his/her role within the SMT for enhancing pupil attainment and achievement

- ✓ Develops, implements, monitors and evaluates school policies for which s/he has been allocated an overview role

- ✓ Sets high standards of behaviour and attendance and a culture of challenge within the curricular stages for which s/he has been allocated responsibility

- ✓ Sets high standards of behaviour and attendance and a culture of challenge within the curricular stages for which s/he has been allocated responsibility

Leading and Developing People: Within a given remit, a senior manager:

- ✓ Develops strategies for professional review and ongoing CPD, including coaching and mentoring, for middle managers in link departments

- ✓ Works with middle managers and class teachers to ensure that there is effective deployment of staff and a team approach to educational provision

- ✓ Supports link middle managers to achieve high standards of performance and takes appropriate action when performance is unsatisfactory

- ✓ Contributes to a collegiate style of working within the SMT and between the SMT and other colleagues.

Leading Change and Improvement: Within a given remit, a senior manager:

- ✓ Works with link middle managers to audit existing stage and departmental policies, plans and procedures at least annually

- ✓ Assists middle managers to draw up stage and departmental action plans, in conjunction with colleagues, to address priorities for improvement in provision

- ✓ Ensures that link middle managers and other colleagues implement plans and monitor progress towards embedding new learning and teaching approaches

- ✓ Works with link middle managers and other colleagues to evaluate the impact of new approaches on classroom practice and pupil performance

Managing Resources: Within a given remit, a senior manager:

- ✓ Ensures that link middle managers and other colleagues distribute allocated resources in line with agreed maintenance and improvement priorities

- ✓ Ensures that link middle managers monitor resources and facilities in order to meet health and safety requirements

- ✓ Ensures that link middle managers and other colleagues remain within budget limits and works with them to evaluate the impact of spending on learning and teaching in terms of cost-effectiveness

In *Lists 2- 4* which follow, use the following HMIE rating scale to indicate your current levels of expertise in the various attributes that are listed:

6 (excellent)

5 (very good)

4 (good)

3(satisfactory)

2(weak)

1(unsatisfactory)

List 2: Professional Values and Personal Commitments: Within a given remit, a senior manager:

- ✓ Articulates a clear vision and ensures that it is shared and understood within his/her area of responsibility

- ✓ Is committed to integrity and ethical practice within his/her area of responsibility with regard to equality, social justice and inclusion

- ✓ Is committed to and encourages due respect for self and others in and across departments

- ✓ Is committed to critical self-evaluation and ongoing professional development and encourages and supports it within his/her area of responsibility

List 3: Knowledge and Understanding: Within a given remit, a senior manager knows and understands:

- ✓ The principles of effective learning and teaching, including the use of new technologies, and how to manage these

- ✓ Local and national priorities and the roles and structures of relevant bodies and their implications for the school

- ✓ Strategies for raising attainment and achieving excellence

- ✓ The principles and practice of team leadership

- ✓ The principles of leading change and policy development and implementation

- ✓ Social trends as they impact on stage, departmental and school plans, policies, aims and methods

- ✓ Self-evaluation and improvement strategies, quality assurance systems and the tools that support an evidence-based approach to decision-making

List 4: Personal Qualities and Interpersonal Skills: A senior manager:

- ✓ Understands and can control personal emotions

- ✓ Understands and can help others control their emotions

- ✓ Creates and maintains a positive atmosphere and team spirit

- ✓ Takes account of the values and views of others, including parents, children and young people

- ✓ Inspires and motivates others

- ✓ Thinks strategically within the relevant area of respons-ibility

- ✓ Uses effective decision-making processes and problem-solving techniques

- ✓ Communicates effectively in terms both of providing information and listening to feedback

- ✓ Shows political insight related to issues of power and influence and a variety of agendas

Critical Incident Analysis

As the name implies, *critical incident analysis* involves the retrospective analysis of how someone handled a given situation in terms of what they did, how they went about it and why. The purpose of the analysis is to provide pointers as to how the person might act next time in a similar situation. In the context of this programme, the process is a useful way of linking the various aspects of the *Standard for Team Leadership* (and the theory that underpins it) to the day-to-day actions of real team leaders as a means of learning.

Case Study

Individually, consider the examples below of how a middle manager or senior manager dealt with a particular situation and was left wondering if he/she might have handled it better.

The first two examples were based on an invitation to the managers in question to select a recent incident that they had to deal with as a leader/manager. The third example was given to them. Using the *Standard for Team Leadership* as a guide, the managers were asked to:

(a) Provide a brief description of the nature of the situation
(b) Briefly describe the steps taken in terms of professional action to deal with the situation
(c) Describe the personal qualities and interpersonal skills that were used
(d) Provide a rationale for the steps that were taken (What kinds of knowledge and understanding were used and which educational values underpinned the actions taken?)
(e) Describe what was learned about leadership and management as a consequence of the situation

Activity WS1.4: Critical Incident Analysis

Individually, set down your views about the action (or lack of action) taken in the situations described on the following pages. The first scenario is relevant to those who aspire to middle management. The second scenario is relevant to those who aspire to senior management. The third scenario is relevant to both. Take about 15-20 minutes to consider the relevant scenario.

You are provided with a series of questions so that you can briefly record your views. Share these with a colleague if possible.

Critical Incident Analysis 1: (Aspiring to middle management):

Provide a brief description of the nature of the situation: A parent phoned to complain to the HT that her daughter had been slapped by another girl in the classroom of one of my colleagues. The parent was particularly aggrieved that the teacher was out of the classroom at the time and wanted assurances of action and no recurrence.

The HT asked me, as line manager, to investigate and deal with the matter, remembering that school policy with regard to teachers not leaving classrooms was perfectly clear. I was to report back to the HT and could seek advice any time if things were getting difficult.

Briefly describe the professional actions you took to deal with the situation:
Spoke to the teacher in question who admitted leaving the room to get some materials that she had left in the base. She said she was quite unaware of any incident. I reminded her of school policy about leaving classrooms. Accepted her point about just being away for a moment but insisted that in future the class should not be left. Interviewed alleged victim and aggressor and other pupils – the aggressor's guilt was clear. She said it was just fun. Spoke to her and made it clear that any recurrence of this behaviour would lead to immediate suspension and a report to parents. I suggested that she should apologise to the victim in front of class and promise no recurrence. I made it clear that I was willing to draw a line under the incident on this occasion so long as apologies were made. An Apology was given and accepted.

I informed HT of what I had done and HT advised parent accordingly.

Which personal qualities and interpersonal skills did you call on?
Sensitivity to concerns of all; communication skills; confidence; problem-solving and decision-making skills; sensitivity to the politics of the situation

Why did you take the steps that you did? (Which educational values influenced you and what kinds of knowledge and understanding did you apply to the situation?)
Commitment to the safety and happiness of all children; willingness to support colleague while reminding her of agreed policies; belief in the value of giving folk a second chance and in the potential power of public admissions of guilt; firmness and clarity in explaining the implications of future recurrence; effort not to over-react and be heavy-handed but conscious of need to provide a clear lead

What would you do in a similar situation next time and why?
Things worked out quite well (in the typical way of children the two girls are now quite friendly) There has been no recurrence of the teacher leaving the room. I think I took the lead in matters, worked well with others to find a solution and communicated well. I think I could learn more about mediation in such situations, especially if there is denial all round.

However a colleague thought that, having spoken to the teacher in question and secured promises about future classroom absence as I did, I should then have left it to her to deal with the situation along the lines that I did before reporting back to me so that I could report to HT in my turn. And a colleague with pastoral duties wanted to know why I had not involved her at any stage before, during or after the incident. Another colleague doubted my wisdom in insisting upon an apology from the guilty party. And one was surprised the HT had not dealt with the matter personally in the first place.

So now I am wondering...

Critical Incident Analysis 2: (Aspiring to senior management)

Provide a brief description of the nature of the situation

As DHT with day-to-day responsibility for implementation of the school's assessment policy, I issued a memo to staff with regard to deadlines for submitting school test results. A certain teacher failed to submit results by the due date and I was concerned that this would lead to a delay in sending reports to parents ahead of a forthcoming parents' night

Briefly describe the professional actions you took to deal with the situation

I went in search of the teacher in question only to discover that she was away being interviewed for a promoted post in another school. I left a memo asking her to contact me as soon as she returned to school. She arrived at my office about an hour later with my memo. I immediately asked her for an explanation about the delayed results. She explained that the previous three nights had been taken up with leadership of an extra-curricular activity that she regularly led, caring for a sick daughter plus preparation for her forthcoming interview. She had expected to finish the reports on time but a last-minute computer glitch had caused a delay. Knowing she would be away at interview, she had asked a colleague to explain matters to me (who then did not) and she hoped to complete the recording of test results later in the day. I pointed out that deadlines had been issued in plenty of time and reminded her of school policy and the importance of keeping faith with parents and children. I also told her that she should be better organised in future. She broke down in tears and left my room without another word. I later discovered that she had been told just before the meeting with me that she had not been successful in her promotion interview.

Which personal qualities and interpersonal skills did you call on?

I was sensitive about a possible delay to important parental information; clear and speedy communication skills; confidence that I had taken the correct steps in issuing and following up the deadlines memo; problem-solving and firm decision-making skills.

Why did you take the steps that you did? (Which educational values influenced you and what kinds of knowledge and understanding did you apply to the situation?)

Commitment to ensuring that agreed school policy was properly implemented; a commitment to speedy, clear face-to-face communication; a commitment to helping colleagues to carry out duties efficiently and effectively; firmness and clarity in explaining the implications of future recurrence; effort not to over-react but conscious of need to provide a clear lead.

What would you do in a similar situation next time and why?

I felt that I was well within my rights to act as I did. Deadlines are deadlines and are there for a reason. Teachers respect a firm manager. However, a colleague of the teacher who came across her distraught in the staffroom told me about the failed interview and complained to the head about my perceived insensitivity and lack of flexibility. The teacher meanwhile resigned from her leadership of the extra-curricular activity. The head interviewed me and said that while it was important to ensure that agreed policies were implemented, she felt that I should have been more sensitive to the overall situation – not least by first asking the teacher how her interview had gone. She also felt that I should have delegated the matter to a middle manager to deal with in the first instance, keeping myself as DHT with overall responsibility in reserve. And she felt that I should apologise to the teacher

So now I am wondering...

Critical Incident Analysis 3 (Aspiring to middle/senior Management):

Analyse the situation below from the perspective of an aspiring middle manager or an aspiring senior manager

Jenny is a bright, happy and conscientious 5th year pupil. She has dreams of being a doctor or lawyer. She got top grades in all her Standard Grades in S4 and was now looking forward to the results of the 5 'Highers' that she sat back in May/June. Her results came in and she was shocked to discover that, although she had scored 3 'A' and 1 'B' passes in four of her exams, she had failed her English and would therefore not secure a place at university. Her parents were even more shocked – and angry – when they made private enquiries through some teacher friends and discovered the following:

The teacher who demanded a 'higher' section as his right was near retirement and seemed to have lost interest over the last year or two. He had also been absent on and off during the year. Class work had been covered in a somewhat perfunctory way and homework had seldom been issued and even more seldom marked and returned. Pupils had been allowed to gossip to one another as they worked and generally waste time. There had been no use of past papers for exam practice.

One parent had complained to the head of department about the teacher in question at a parents' reporting night earlier in the session, having heard of his poor reputation, but had been assured that results of prelims from the class were overall 'as expected'. Another parent had mentioned the lack of homework and marking from the teacher to her son's pastoral teacher but nothing seemed to have happened. Certainly Jenny could confirm that neither the head of department nor any member of the senior management team or pastoral staff had ever visited her class. Jenny admitted that homework was seldom issued or marked but had never mentioned this to her parents as she thought she would be OK.

Other pupils in the group had also done less well than expected though three of Jenny's class mates who were similar to her in ability had scored 'A' passes in higher English. It turned out that they had been getting private tutoring throughout. A teacher admitted to Jenny's mum that the head of department had allocated Jenny's group to the teacher in question to please him while she took the bottom set, hoping that Jenny and company would be bright enough to get there anyway. A member of the school senior management team who was linked to the department was aware of this and had apparently accepted the situation.

Critical Incident Analysis

Use the questions provided below to jot down your responses to whichever scenarios(s) you tackled. If possible, share them with some colleagues.

The nature of the situation: What preliminary thoughts and ideas would you have had about dealing with this situation?

Professional action to deal with the situation: Any comment on the actions that were taken/not taken?

Personal qualities and interpersonal skills: Did the manager(s) make good use of these?

Educational values and kinds of knowledge and understanding: Did the manager(s) make good use of these?

Dealing with a similar situation next time and why: If given another chance, what should the manager(s) do next time and why?

Feedback

Introduction

In this section of each workshop session, the feedback that is provided comprises information about the views of previous readers and findings from research concerning the topics in focus. It is then for each participant to decide how relevant the feedback is to her or his particular situation. Feedback for middle managers and senior managers is differentiated in the case of some activities; in others the feedback is generic in nature. We begin with feedback for aspiring middle managers with regard to activities WS1.1 – WS1.3, followed by feedback for aspiring senior managers with regard to the same activities and then feedback for both categories with regard to Activity WS1.4

Feedback: Activity WS1.1: Key Distinctions (aspiring middle managers)

Excellent *teachers* and excellent *leaders* of teachers

It may be that *leadership and management* qualities have more on common with *learning and teaching* qualities than is sometimes appreciated. Some 20 years ago, an HMIE report on effective schools in Scotland noted the personal qualities of effective *teachers* as follows:

Characteristics such as patience, enthusiasm, tolerance and understanding assist teachers to achieve a good rapport with pupils. When teachers see pupils as individuals, show a genuine interest in what they say, write and do, demonstrate that their contributions are valued and taken seriously and give encouragement and praise where due, pupils respond positively and are more willing to commit themselves and take an active part in their own learning. A distinguishing characteristic of effective teachers, therefore, is their ability to create a climate of confidence and trust and to win the respect of pupils. Personal qualities of fairness, firmness and calm control contribute to that atmosphere of purpose which is a prerequisite for sound learning.
(*Effective Secondary Schools*, HMI, 1988)

Now substitute references to *teachers* with *'leaders'*, references to *pupils* with *'colleagues'* and references to *learning* with *'development'*:

Characteristics such as patience, enthusiasm, tolerance and under-

41

standing assist leaders to achieve a good rapport with colleagues. When leaders see colleagues as individuals, show a genuine interest in what they say, write and do, demonstrate that their contributions are valued and taken seriously and give encouragement and praise where due, colleagues respond positively and are more willing to commit themselves and take an active part in their own development. A distinguishing characteristic of effective leaders, therefore, is their ability to create a climate of confidence and trust and to win the respect of colleagues. Personal qualities of fairness, firmness and calm control contribute to that atmosphere of purpose which is a prerequisite for sound development.

A fair description of leadership, it would seem. Clearly, leaders and teachers have much in common, not least in terms of people skills.

But if leadership is essentially about working with and through other people to achieve objectives then, as *Thought Pieces 1.3 and 1.4* make clear, whereas success as a teacher depends on using one's *personal* expertise, success as a leader depends on being able to motivate other adults and to harness the expertise of *others*, to point it in the right direction and then to develop a team approach to overcoming challenges.

Feedback Activity W1.2: Leaders or managers? (Aspiring middle managers)

Profession actions most commonly associated with leadership include:

Visioning, inspiring, motivating, being sensitive, teambuilding, climate-setting, empowering, strategic thinking, transforming, taking decisions.

Professional actions most commonly associated with management are:

Auditing, analysing, planning, problem solving, organising, selecting, developing, delegating, implementing, monitoring, budgeting, evaluating

Leadership and management are, of course, both important as the following comments affirm.

Leadership is about doing the *right thing; management is about doing the thing right*

(Bennis, W and Nanus, B (1985) *Leaders*

Visioning without planning is merely dreaming

Planning without visioning is merely passing the time

Visioning combined with planning can change the world.

(Barker, J. A (1990) The Power of Vision

Feedback: Activity WS1.3: Self-evaluation (Middle and senior managers versions)

Clearly, the outcomes of self-evaluation depend upon individual circumstances. *The Standard* is useful for taking a snap view of where your development priorities lie. But snap views that do not take other perspectives into consideration may be flawed. At worst, self-evaluation can become self-delusion, unless the individual is also willing to consider the views of others – and then probe more deeply. Review your self-evaluation at the end of the input sessions as part of preparing a personal learning plan (Session 5).

Feedback: Activity WS1.1: Role differences (Aspiring senior managers)

(a) For new senior managers there is always the challenge to their confidence and courage of suddenly having to operate outside their former comfort zones and securing the support of colleagues who are experts in their own field. Winning the respect and trust of such experts is a major challenge. All of a sudden the subject expertise, and associated credibility, of aspiring senior managers may no longer matter so much as they may no longer even have teaching duties and are now dealing with colleagues with other subject expertise.

In terms of *functions*, the senior manager has the same fundamental responsibility for harnessing and directing the work of colleagues towards raising pupil attainment as a head of department or similar middle manager. In the case of the senior manager, 'colleagues' are likely to include departmental and pastoral leaders, parents, supporting agencies, other schools and local authority officers in a bigger picture, 'joined up' whole school approach to addressing pupil needs.

The new senior manager is also likely to be faced with a much greater variety of day-to-day tasks, some calling for leadership,

43

some calling for management and some calling for administrative skills. So time management and the ordering of priorities become more important.

Depending on their remit, senior managers will need the knowledge and skills associated with the likes of timetabling and curricular design.

(b) So far as *qualities* are concerned, the senior manager and the middle manager are likely to share most if not all of the same *values* and many of the same *interpersonal skills*. With regard to *values*, some senior managers, usually from the secondary sector, declare that they became more 'pupil-centred' and less 'subject-centred' once they joined the senior management team. They felt they were more concerned with the overall impact on the pupil of a *range* of teaching demands across the curriculum whereas previously as departmental heads their focus was on the teaching demands relevant to their subject.

So far as *interpersonal skills* are concerned, a senior manager, especially in the secondary sector, will be responsible for building cross- curricular teamwork rather than departmental or stage teamwork. Securing the commitment of a group of middle managers to a common whole school objective is arguably more challenging than securing the commitment of a range of like-minded subject colleagues to a given subject priority.

Being ready to support colleagues with time and being ready to 'roll up their sleeves' and be out and about in the school rather than sitting in offices and drafting memos and policy papers will assist senior managers to secure new levels of credibility with hard-pressed middle managers and other colleagues.

Finally, the decisions taken by a senior manager, seeking to find a due balance of overall impact on pupils of different subject priorities, may well be different from the decisions that the same senior manager might have taken as a departmental head.

Activity WS1.2: Management, administration, leadership, teaching (senior managers)

Both the remit of the DHT and the activity log throw up a number of points about the *potential* of the DHT to promote learning and teaching, although a mere reading of the remit or of the diary of activities does not of itself provide any indications of the quality of input.

First, the fact that there seem to be three times a week when the SMT meet to discuss strategic issues – and are invited to comment on specific proposals – certainly suggests that the DHT has the opportunity to contribute to overall direction and strategy for school improvement. There seems to be scope too for the DHT to influence what is happening in the classroom in and through his/her presence at departmental meetings and in meetings with individual teachers. Again there is indirect opportunity for the DHT to influence the quality of what is happening in terms of the school's CPD programme, PSD programme and NQT programme. The DHT clearly does not hesitate to grasp the nettle of difficult situations.

Close work with support staff indicates considerable potential for the DHT to promote a spirit of collegiality throughout the school to the benefit of all. And the readiness to meet parents and to contact other agencies suggests a willingness to look outwards as well as inwards for solutions.

There is evidence of leadership by example in terms of the DHT's high profile among pupils at interval and lunch-time and in the amount of time
that is devoted to helping individual students to complete UCAS forms. Arguably, however, taking on a number of such interviews, with the associated time to read over drafts, should be delegated to pastoral staff, student tutors and the like, with the DHT retaining an overview.

Most of the activities come under the heading of management but that is to be expected as any remit is going to be largely about the day-to-day management of tasks that relate to the implementation of the school's vision. It can take a few moments to enunciate a vision – and a lifetime to achieve it. With regard to day-to-day management, however, the 'message' about what the DHT is doing seems to be more about challenge and support rather than about naming, blaming and shaming and that should certainly promote learning.

Finally, although the DHT does devote quite a bit of time to admin, the type of admin involved tends to be an inevitable concomitant of the leadership and management that is going on – and is consigned to times outside the school working day whenever possible.

Overall, there is reason to believe that the professional activities of this DHT reflect a reasonable mixture of leadership, management and administrative activity.

Feedback: Activity WS1.3: A Standard for Team Leadership: Self-evaluation (senior managers)

As already noted in the case of aspiring middle managers, the outcomes of self-evaluation depend upon individual circumstances. As before, it is worth reviewing self-evaluations at the end of the input sessions and prior to preparing any project and learning plans.

Feedback: Activity WS1.4: Critical Incident Analysis (Aspiring middle/senior managers)

The case studies overall make clear the need for a 'joined up' team approach to dealing with issues based on agreed values, policies, systems, structures, procedures and a culture of mutual support.

Among the specific points that **Critical Incident 1** has thrown up among readers in the past are the following:

(a)   The decision of the HT to delegate the enquiry. Some argue that the HT should have conducted the enquiry personally, having been the one to receive the complaint. The majority think the HT was right to delegate. The general feeling was that complaints should be resolved at the lowest possible level.

(b)   All commentators wanted to be assured that the line manager had discussed the policy issues with the teacher in private and not in front of the class. Most people think that the line manager should have left things to the class teacher to sort things out – or at least offered the teacher the opportunity to sort things out. The overall feeling here was that the line manager should have been willing to delegate to the teacher in the same way that the HT had delegated to the line manager in the first place.

(c)   Some think the line manager was right to seek a public apology from the culprit as part of reparation and moving on. The majority feel that that aspect should have been dealt with in private and that the line manager risked refusal and further confrontation.

(d)   Some feel the line manager was quite right to move quickly without consulting others. Others feel that advice should have been sought first from pastoral personnel to see if there were any patterns of misbehaviour – and information should certainly have been sent on afterwards to those personnel.

(e)   There has also been some discussion about the policy about leaving classrooms as sometimes this is unavoidable.

Critical Incident 2

Most previous commentators on this scenario felt that many of the actions and motives of the DHT were entirely proper. It was important to ensure that the school's agreed policy on assessment and reporting was implemented in good time ahead of a parents' night. Again, the DHT had quite rightly issued a memo about due dates and quite rightly followed it up with a specific enquiry about missing data.

But the manner of the treatment of the colleague in question by the DHT left much to be desired. Most commentators felt that the DHT in this scenario had forgotten one of the fundamental rules of leadership. If you focus on achieving tasks and results without giving much thought to the needs of the colleagues whose contribution is so vital to the achievement of those tasks and results, then there is a very good chance that you will fail to achieve the outcomes that you seek.

It would have cost the DHT nothing to begin by enquiring about the teacher's interview and then commiserating with the teacher before seeking reasons for the non-submission of the class assessments. The reasons provided were legitimate enough and did not sound like empty excuses. The DHT could then have settled for 'a word to the wise' and urged speedy submission of the required information, rather than the abrupt, insensitive way in which the matter was dealt with. The points made in *Thought Piece 1.2* are very relevant here. Senior mangers treat their colleagues merely as post-holders and not as people at their peril.

Critical Incident 3

Situations like this one are worryingly common. They reflect what can only be described as a total lack of leadership and management. What we see here is a laisser-faire approach to management with individual teachers left to their own devices and little or no challenge or support provided. The issues are being avoided. This might be fine where the teachers in question are fully committed, although even in such cases a team approach, involving many good teachers, is even more powerful.

Among the specific points most frequently made by previous readers are the following:

The teacher in question should be thoroughly ashamed of himself. He should have sought help and declined the opportunity to take such a vital class group instead of seeing it as some sort of right.

There does not seem to be an agreed policy on learning and teaching in place or any agreed means of monitoring and evaluating its implementation. Questions should be asked of the head teacher.

The dropping levels of commitment by the teacher in question should have been addressed some time earlier with appropriate support from the head of department. Appropriate disciplinary action should also have been considered by the head teacher.

As an act of damage limitation, the teacher should not have been allocated such a vital teaching group – and certainly not on a full-time basis. The head of department and DHT were at fault here in bowing to the wishes of the teacher rather than prioritising the needs of the pupils.

The head of department should have investigated complaints much more thoroughly – as should have the pastoral teacher, with appropriate action to follow.

There should have been visits by senior managers to the classroom of the teacher in line with agreed policy on monitoring and evaluation.

Workshop Session 2: Culture and ethos; values and vision

Workshop Session 2: Culture and ethos; values and vision

1. Introduction

We begin with a definition of terms. The concepts of 'culture' and 'ethos' are sometimes spoken of as if they are synonymous. But there is practical value in distinguishing between them. In this programme, 'culture' is taken to be the long established norms, rites, rituals and procedures whereby a school traditionally goes about its business. Culture, so defined, is deep-seated and people may not even be aware of its controlling impact on their lives. But in essence it describes the status quo or 'the way we do things around here' - particularly as leaders and managers, given the focus of this development programme.

Few leaders or managers are given the opportunity to develop a culture from scratch in a new school or department. But they disregard the established culture of a school at their peril if they hope to bring about change and improvement. The status quo is the biggest obstacle to any change, not least if an aspiring leader fails to recognise the nature of the status quo and its importance. Looking at a school's culture is therefore a critical first step towards bringing about improvement in the way any school goes about its business.

By contrast the 'ethos' of a school is the set of relationships that exist currently in a school, partly because of traditional cultural imperatives but also to a large extent because of the leadership and management style of the current group of leaders. The concept of ethos is closely related to the 'climate' of a school in terms of the 'warmth' or 'coldness' of relationships. Ethos and climate will depend on the values that leaders bring into the existing culture.

We speak of knowledge, skills and values. But the greatest of these is values. Values will certainly influence a leader's vision of what effective education provision should look like in their school or departments and they will also influence the way in which a given leader goes about translating that vision into reality - and quite possibly bringing in a new kind of culture along the way. If new leaders hope to influence others, however, it is essential first for them to be ready to articulate and explain their stand on issues.

At the same time, as with the established culture, leaders need to identify and respect the values of others if they are to secure their commitment in trying to achieve some shared objective.

In this session, readers are invited to reflect on and analyse the culture, the ethos, the vision and the values of a school that they know (not necessarily their current school) and their implications for improvement. Then they are invited to reflect on their own values particularly with regard to leading a school-based improvement project.

Learning Outcomes

By the end of this workshop session readers will have:

✓ Read a number of thought pieces related to culture, ethos, vision and values
✓ Analysed the culture of a school that they know
✓ Reflected upon their personal values and vision
✓ Expressed personal values and aims in connection with any proposed school improvement project

Workshop Session2: Culture and ethos; values and vision

Thought Piece 2.1: Culture and change

Culture can be defined as an amalgam of the values, norms and beliefs that characterise the way in which a group of people behave within a specific organisational setting. It has been summed up as 'the way we do things around here'. There are various ways of characterising school culture. We look here at two such ways. In the first we look at school culture in terms of different leadership and management strategies. In the second we look at four types of school culture in relation to staff attitudes to change.

2.1.1. Leadership and management cultures

Charles Handy and others in the 1990s identified common types of culture that might exist in a school and that leaders would have to take account of if they wanted to ascertain the extent to which a given type of culture might facilitate change.

(a) The role culture

Management is traditional and hierarchical. There are clear job descriptions and roles, formalised top-down communications and procedures. Control is exerted by the head or a narrow band of senior managers. There is a focus on efficiency.

(b) The club culture

The head teacher cultivates the support of like-minded colleagues.

Circles or cliques of intimates develop and have greater influence than formal post holders who fall outside the club. The head is likely to use power in an arbitrary way rather than follow agreed procedures. Decisions are often made informally with the 'in-crowd' and little is written down.

(c) The person culture

In this culture individuals are allowed to display their talents and managers interfere as little as possible, leaving the experts to get on with the job. Teachers are persuaded, influenced and bargained with but not commanded or instructed. In short, teachers are pretty well autonomous and managers hesitate to challenge them or their performances.

(d) The balkanised culture

In balkanised schools, teachers develop loyalty to their own group and there is competition between groups, encouraged by the head. Inter-departmental conflict over resources is common and there are distinct sub-cultures that make working towards a common ethos difficult. School leaders and teacher representatives are often at odds with each other.

(e) The collaborative culture

In such a culture there is a clear and shared vision about the values and purposes of the school and this vision and the ways of achieving it are regularly reviewed. There is a high commitment to teamwork both within and between departments and between the various levels of management. Not only are all teachers invited to contribute to proposals for the future direction of the school, but support staff, pupils and their parents are given an important voice in the decision-making process.

Thought Piece 2.1.2: Attitudes to change

The work of Susan Rosenholz and others in the 1990s is important as it focuses on how staff attitudes can have such a major impact on the possibility of change. She identified four types of staff/school attitudes:

(a) The stuck school or department.

Staff are not much interested in change. Things are said to have been tried before and always failed. Staff believe that the nature of the catchment area constrains what can be achieved and there is a feeling of powerlessness. External priorities predominate so there is not much point in getting into discussions about personal priorities for change.

(b) The wandering school.

Many different innovations are started but then they are not persevered with. There is a number of enthusiastic individuals but they are all pursuing their own agendas without any coherent plan or focus. There is a sense of innovation overload

(c) The promenading school.

Here change is felt to be unnecessary because the school has a history of impressive achievements, not least in terms of examination performance. Placement requests into the school are high. Staff are well into their comfort zones and see no need for change, given the level of success

(d) The moving school.

Here there is a healthy blend of change and stability. There is an acceptance of change and a desire for continuous improvement. The direction of the school or department is discussed by all staff. In terms of development, the staff are clear about where they are, where they are going and why.

It is not uncommon to find elements of different management strategies in the same school – or elements of different attitudes to change. And even if there are some poor management practices and some poor staff attitudes, there is a great deal of evidence to show that individual departments or stages and even individual teachers can thrive, working in ways that are more effective and which result in higher achievement levels for their students.

Thought Piece 2.2: Code of Practice on Collegiality

Establishing a culture of collegiality in schools is considered to be so vital that it is now a condition of service that all teachers should contribute to the creation of such a culture. The following extract *(in italics)* from the code of practice, focusing on collegiality at school level, is taken directly from Part 1: Appendix 1.4 of the SNCT *Handbook of Conditions of Service* issued in 2007. The full handbook is available online at www.snct.org.uk

Introduction

Collegiality is at the heart of the National Agreement "A Teaching Profession for the 21st Century". Collegiality is a process and a way of working which reflects on relationships and participation by all staff on all aspects of school life.

Collegiality depends on the existence of a climate of professional trust among the Scottish Executive Education Department, councils, directorates, school managers and school staff.

Effective collegiality will not only enhance and develop teacher professionalism; it will also enhance the learning and teaching environment in Scottish schools.

Collegiality at council and school levels can only exist in a climate where the views of all staff are valued and respected, where staff views are fully considered and where staff feel able to contribute to decisions on all areas of school life comfortably, openly and with dignity and where workload issues are recognised. Where such a climate exists, staff are fully involved in contributing to the life of the school and the council.

Although councils and schools will be at various stages in the development of a collegiate culture, LNCTs and establishments should have made some movement in the direction of collegiate working as part of the process of implementation of the National Agreement.

The benefits which accrue from collegiality are not only improved industrial relations and professional satisfaction for teachers, but also an enhanced environment for learning and teaching. The ultimate beneficiaries of collegiality are therefore the young people who attend school.

There is no single model of collegiality but the following description of good practice should be used by staff at all levels to guide and evaluate progress towards collegiate working. It is also important that time is allocated for purposeful and positive involvement in decision making and for engagement in collegiate activities...

Collegiality at School Level

In schools, collegiate working is carried out within the context of the 35 hour working week.

It is also important to acknowledge that every school is different and that no single model of collegiality will apply to all schools. For instance, the practicalities of collegiate working in a two or three teacher primary school will be very different from working arrangements in a secondary school with a pupil roll of 1600 and over 100 teaching staff. Nevertheless, certain common principles should apply and what follows is a description of the collegiate school.

Strong, effective communications operate within the collegiate school. The prevailing atmosphere fosters mutual respect and encourages frank, open and honest communications amongst all staff. There is evidence of a range of meetings including meetings involving the school's management team and representatives of the staff as a whole and which may include representatives of trade unions and professional organisations. The outcomes of such meetings are communicated to all relevant staff.

All staff contribute to the construction of the Working Time Agreement through a process of consultation, professional dialogue and negotiation; consequently, all staff have a sense of ownership of the Agreement. The Agreement is transparent, is signed by all members of the school negotiating team and is submitted to the LNCT by the specified date. Once finalised, the terms of the Agreement are respected by all members of staff and inform the work of the school over the session to which the Agreement applies.

All staff members recognise their responsibility to contribute to the school development process and to participate in this process in a collegiate and constructive manner. There are clear mechanisms in place to allow staff to make their views known; staff express their views openly and professionally. The opinions of staff are valued and are used as input to the school's development plan and policy development processes. School policies and decisions are regularly reviewed and all staff participate in the review process. Any changes required to the plan during the session are subject to appropriate consultation and take account of teacher workload.

Within the context of the 35 hour week and Working Time Agreements all staff in the collegiate school participate in a wide range of whole school activities, such as school committees, policy formulation, curriculum development, professional development and additional supervised pupil activity.

In the collegiate school, leadership qualities are evident throughout the school. There is a devolved and participative style of leadership *and management. Staff are afforded opportunities to develop leadership skills and take advantage of these opportunities. Leadership in this context is distinct from management duties as set out in Part 2, Section 2 (Main Duties) of the National Scheme and Annex B of the National Agreement.*

The collegiate school utilises and develops the skills, talents and interests of all staff and involves all staff in the key decisions affecting the life of the school as a whole. More broadly, the spirit of collegiality extends beyond teachers and support staff, and includes parents, pupils and partner agencies.

There are clear links between the notion of collegiality and participatory and distributed leadership. As the Circular notes:

In the collegiate school, leadership qualities are evident throughout the school. There is a devolved and participative style of leadership and management. Staff are afforded opportunities to develop leadership skills and take advantage of these opportunities.

So far, so good. But what if a climate of collegial trust does not exist in a school, stage or department? After all, such a climate cannot simply be mandated. Close reading of school inspection reports indicates that there are still a number of schools where staff on either side of the school management-workforce 'divide' behave in ways that consciously or unconsciously militate against the creation of a climate of trust in which collegiate working may thrive. And there is, of course, the fact that the very existence of hierarchical structures in a school militates against collegial working, not least given the salary differentials involved in a range of job-sized posts. Variations in non-contact time do not help either.

As always, it is up to school leaders and those who aspire to school leadership to take the initiative. They could do worse than to follow the advice contained in the Circular – constantly emphasising the importance of mutual respect, creating strong and effective communication systems, encouraging frank, open and honest debate, involving staff in the decision – making process, providing leadership opportunities for all staff and ensuring that resources and time are shared among all staff as equitably as possible.

Yet staff too must share responsibility for creating a climate of collegial cooperation. Indeed the frequent recurrence of phrases such as 'the staff as a whole' and 'all staff' within the Circular, not least with regard to working time agreements, makes it clear that all staff have a duty, enshrined in their conditions of service, to participate in a collegial approach to improving attainment and achievement that takes due account of teacher workload.

School leaders in their turn should ensure that all staff can have the opportunity to comment on planning and policy proposals, even although it is likely that draft proposals will have been drawn up by small representative working groups. And wise leaders will ensure that even when plans and policies are implemented, they will be monitored and evaluated by all staff to see if they are having the desired impact – and revised if they are not.

Thought Piece 2.3: Learning Organisations

In his book, *'The Fifth Discipline'* (1990), Peter Senge, an extremely influential thinker, described the nature of a learning organisation as follows:

- People seek continually to expand their capacity to achieve results

- Fresh and open thinking is encouraged

- People always aspire to better, individually and collectively

- People are continually learning how to learn together

- The integrated nature of all of the above is recognised

In such an organisation, the climate and culture is such that members feel valued, respected and appreciated. The leader facilitates team learning and the communication processes encourage full participation, with everyone feeling that their suggestions will be considered and will help to shape improvement plans. The leader seeks a shared vision and models the behaviour that is encouraged.

In a learning organisation there is always a creative tension between the vision of a better future and current reality. Such creative tension can be reduced either by moving the vision towards current reality or by moving current reality towards the vision. Effective leaders, having engaged everyone in establishing the vision in the first place, choose the latter.

Senge's description of a learning organisation applies to any organisation. It certainly applies to schools. Schools which reflect his principles seem to achieve high standards of pupil performance.

Thought Piece 2.4 From Values to objectives

Values are in essence those personal beliefs about what are the important things in life. They explain why we behave as we do (although sometimes our behaviour contradicts our declared values) Educational values are concerned with what we believe and do if we are to be good teachers or leaders. Such values are likely to be themselves underpinned by our professional morals or ethics. What are our beliefs about right and wrong in education? What constitutes proper professional behaviour in an educationalist? Finally our views about right and wrong and ethical behaviour are likely to be influenced by our personal deep - seated beliefs about the ultimate issues of life: Who am I? Where do I come from? Why am I here? Where am I going? In a profession such as teaching it is very difficult to separate our professional and our personal values.

Vision is a mental picture of a preferred future in which things are in some way better than they are now (the definition of 'better' being dependent on our core values in the first place) Think of the famous speech of Martin Luther King, 'I have a dream'. Or think of the differences in pupil performance that you envisage will be the outcome of your chosen project. Having a vision of a desired future invests with meaning the tasks that will have to be undertaken if the vision is to be realised. By the same token, carrying out tasks may well help retrospectively to clarify the vision in the first place. A vision implies some sort of dissatisfaction with the current state of affairs and is a catalyst for action.

A vision statement or mission statement is the term we apply to the articulation of a vision. It is a succinct summing up of the fundamental raison d'etre of an organisation, an encapsulation of why-we-are-here and what-we-hope-to-achieve. It also conveys the direction in which a school needs to move.

Aims are statements that in effect break down the mission statement into manageable parts. In the case of schools or departments, they are the general declarations of what a school hopes to accomplish in terms of key aspects of its educational provision. In recent years it has become common for schools to draw up lists of six or seven aims that reflect the five national priorities or the nine key areas of provision identified in How Good Is Our School? or a combination of these. In other cases aims have been more closely related to the particular needs of schools in particular contexts.

Objectives are precise declarations of what a school or department hopes to achieve in terms of any particular general aim. In contrast to vision and mission and aims, objectives express functional targets that the school or a group within the school wishes to achieve by the end of the session with regard to pupil learning, attendance rates, behavioural issues and the like. The power of an objective is not so much its inspirational force, as with vision and mission, but in its ability to focus the attention of people on a limited frame of activity.

Taken together, values, vision, aims and objectives reflect the culture or context within which specific priorities for school improvement may be identified and action plans for their achievement can be drawn up.

Thought Piece 2.5: Vision, values and practice: the implications for school leaders

The most successful school leaders invariably have a clear sense of vision and purpose that they can articulate and share with equal clarity. And their vision and sense of purpose underpin the way they go about the every day challenges of their leadership role. Yet the very concept of vision sometimes gets a bad name and can be associated with fanaticism and abnormal behaviour.

It is all the more important then to make it clear that by vision we simply mean a mental image of a realistic and desirable future for the kind of school that the leaders within it are trying to create. Vision is about the aspirations that you have – for yourself, for your pupils, for the kind of leadership that you would like to see, for the kind of learning and teaching that you would like to promote and above all for the kind of culture that you would like to encourage in your school.

Such aspirations are invariably based upon the values that leaders bring to what is inevitably a moral enterprise. It is for that reason that leaders should attempt to reflect consciously on their personal values in education. Such personal reflection is the first step in seeking the commitment of others to share those values and hence that vision. Yet defining our beliefs, our attitudes, our assumptions – and not least our prejudices – is a difficult, daunting task. We all have values but as often as not they lie dormant and we may even avoid expressing them for fear of causing offence or conflict. This is all the more reason to assert that values need to be articulated and debated if they are to achieve anything.

Concerning the commitment of others, it is vital for any leader to remember that classroom teachers too have a vision of what they would like to achieve, underpinned by their own enduring values about what constitutes effective learning and teaching. As Michael Fullan reminds us elsewhere, change cannot be mandated from outside. Certainly there are some non-negotiable aspects of education provision, not least concerning aspects of health and safety and other legal and statutory requirements. Every teacher has a contract of employment that sets out certain fundamental duties and leaders may well from time to time need to remind some of their colleagues of that fact. But it is also important for every leader to remember that the majority of what schools achieve depends upon what happens in the individual classrooms of individual teachers. So leaders rely enormously on the discretion of their teaching colleagues for the delivery of the school or departmental vision.

That being the case, wise leaders not only express their own vision and values for the school but provide opportunities for staff to contribute their values and views to the vision-building process. Leaders should give particular consideration the views not least of those colleagues upon whom you will be calling to implement the vision. There are several dangers in promoting a vision laid down by only one person:

- A single vision may be resisted by others
- The individual's vision relegates others to a passive role
- The vision may leave when the individual leaves

Accordingly leaders should make vision building a collective enterprise. Increasingly too in recent years, leaders have been thorough in providing opportunities for the voice of pupils and parents to be heard in these discussions.

It is also important to appreciate that *visioning*, as opposed to setting out a vision or mission statement is an active ongoing process. School research indicates that it is quite possible not to have a fully articulated vision of a desired future at all *at the start* of a change process. As the planning process and the implementation of the plans get underway, it is entirely probable that the vision will become clearer over time.

The importance of this was nicely expressed some years ago by an executive from Cadbury's who said that the change process was more 'ready, fire, aim' than it was 'ready, aim, fire'.

The danger with 'ready, aim, fire' is that it can become 'ready, aim,

aim', sometimes called paralysis by analysis. On the other hand it is important in visioning to avoid 'ready, fire, fire,' – sometimes known as the Rambo approach to visioning. What is required is an ongoing adjustment between aiming and firing if the target is to be hit. These points also relate to the various stages of the planning process that are dealt with later.

Values and practice

Happily, teachers share much in common with regard to their fundamental values and vision, as should become clear during this leadership development programme. Where the differences appear is in the debates about the precise ways in which the vision may be achieved and the values reflected. Every teacher places a high value on the ability of children to be able to read and write and every teacher has a vision of every child being functionally literate. Yet the methods of Teacher A may be quite different from the methods of Teacher B depending on the different approaches being used to the teaching of reading.

Again, every teacher believes in the value to learning of an orderly environment but Teacher A might be a traditionally strict disciplinarian when it comes to dealing with pupil behaviour and Teacher B might believe in promoting positive behaviour rather than punishing bad behaviour. Every teacher believes that every child should be given the opportunity to realise her or his full potential. But will this be best achieved by streamed, setted or mixed ability teaching groups? And so it goes on.

Diversity versus conformity

There is, of course, a dilemma here for leaders as they contemplate the implications of diverse practice that is based on an essentially similar vision underpinned by essentially similar values. Quite simply, how much diversity of practice can leaders tolerate? There is an argument that says that such diversity of practice is to be welcomed so long as the overarching aims of effective learning and teaching, care and control of pupils and raised achievement are addressed. Certainly it seems likely that teachers will be more comfortable and therefore more effective if they are using approaches to learning and teaching which reflect their own vision and values rather than those of someone else. In the past, it was not uncommon to find schools where clashes of vision and values and diversity of practice were taken for granted and even applauded. Leaders in such schools were wary of insisting upon conformity as they did not want to offend professional sensibilities and cause conflict.

On the other hand, a coherent vision and mission for a school does imply a measure of consistency and coherence of approach across the curriculum. Analysis of effective learning and teaching practices suggests a consistency in the principles that underlie such practice. Studies where pupils were shadowed across the curriculum for a period of time indicate that diversity of practice can cause confusion for pupils which then impacts upon their learning. There is also the harsh reality that what constitutes school effectiveness is increasingly defined by all sorts of public statistics that cover almost every aspect of school life, not least pupil performance in national examinations. Public expectations of educational outcomes and increased levels of public accountability tend to lead to a greater conformity of approach to educational provision.

Implications for leadership practice

All of this has considerable implications for the ways in which leaders develop and sustain a vision for a better future for their schools.

First they must question themselves frequently and thoroughly about their own vision and values and those of their school. Then they must stand ready to express their views verbally and in written form to staff, parents and pupils and to all other stakeholders. This is particularly the case in times of change. Leaders need to explain how any given change will reflect the vision and values of the school – or possibly necessitate a review of that vision and those values.

Annual reviews of vision and value statements should be conducted anyway and staff, parents and pupils alike should be invited to comment on the extent to which the statements reflect the reality of day-to-day practice. At the same time, while encouraging others to express their own values, especially about what constitutes effective learning and teaching, leaders must stand ready to explain why certain views may have to be rejected for the sake of the greater good of the education of the child.

Leaders also need to be clear about those aspects of education provision that are not up for debate. Indeed there is nothing more destructive than to conduct consultations about values and practices that are simply non-negotiable in the first place.

Finally, it is essential for leaders constantly to be analysing those elements of a school's vision and values that are considered to be enduring. If a school has a stated vision such as, 'We are committed to the education of the whole child' or 'We are committed to developing the potential of every child' then school leaders must be ready to interrogate themselves and others about what this means to the school's approach to learning and teaching, how these values directly shape daily practice and what the evidence is to show that the practice is working.

If the vision of a school's desired and realistic future is not being implemented in practice then it is meaningless. The life of the school must embody its vision and bring it alive. School leaders are the catalysts of that embodiment. Leadership without vision means such a reliance on ad hoc solutions that no planning for meaningful futures is possible.

Thought Piece 2.6: Key Commitments of the professional

Michael Eraut (1994) in *Developing Professional Knowledge and Competence'* identifies the following key commitments as the mark of the professional:

- A moral commitment to serve the interests of clients
- An obligation to self-monitor and to periodically review the effectiveness of one's practice
- An obligation to expand one's repertoire, to reflect on one's experience and develop one's expertise
- An obligation that is professional as well as contractual to contribute to the quality of one's organisation
- An obligation to reflect upon and contribute to discussions about the changing role of one's profession in the wider society

These key commitments are the mark of any professional. But they seem particularly relevant to the teaching profession.

This concludes the thought pieces for this workshop session. But see the bibliography for further reading.

Session 2: Workshop Activities

NB. The activities in this session are designed for aspiring middle and senior managers alike. In the case of **Activity WS 2.2**, however, aspiring middle managers are invited to respond in terms of *departmental* mission statements and aims and aspiring senior managers are invited to respond in terms of *whole school* mission statements and aims.

Activity WS2.1: School Cultures

Look again at *Thought Pieces 2.1.1 and 2.1.2.* Individually note down which *one* of the five management 'cultures' and which *one* of the four sets of staff attitudes as described in those thought pieces most closely resembles the management culture and staff attitudes in a school of your choice. Jot down any example of a change initiative that succeeded or foundered as a consequence of the prevailing attitudes or management culture. Which kind of culture and which set of attitudes are most likely to facilitate change? Share your views if possible.

Activity WS2.2: Mission and Aims

It has been claimed that mission or vision building is the strongest and most consistent avenue of influence that school leaders use to enhance student achievement. Quite a claim! So how much mission/vision building is going on in a school/department of your choice?

(a) Provide brief answers to the questions that follow.

   i.   Does the school /department have a vision or mission statement?

   ii. How was it formulated?

   iii. How well is it known?

   iv. To what extent does it have an impact on aims, policies, plans and priorities?

Share your views with colleagues if possible.

(b) Tick the statement in the list that follows that most closely describes the current situation in a school/department of your choice with regard to *aims.*

What is gained or lost as a consequence in terms of managing change?

Our School /Departmental Aims

1. We value education but we do not actually have an agreed written set of aims

2. We have a set of written aims drawn up and issued by the HT/ head of department but they are seldom referred to

3. We developed an agreed set of written aims some time ago but seldom revisit them. Their impact on activities is variable

4. We regularly discuss aims and objectives in groups without necessarily writing them all down. But they do help to direct our activities

5. We developed our set of written aims through discussion among colleagues. They focus on outcomes and reflect national and local priorities. They give direction to our planning

6. Our written and published aims were developed in consultation with, and are known by, colleagues, parents and pupils. We revisit them each year as a starting point for celebrating success and for identifying and implementing improvement priorities

Activity WS2.3: Prioritising values

Prioritising values is a means of identifying for ourselves the values that drive us most of all and is a first step in motivating others.

In this activity you are invited individually to prioritise your own values from each of 4 sets of values that are provided. Share your conclusions if possible with other colleagues to identify similarities and differences of choice.

The 4 sets of values are related to the following:

1. Reasons for becoming a teacher
2. Factors that would influence your choice of school for children of your own
3. Leadership attributes that you would like people to ascribe to you
4. Aspects of leadership style among senior colleagues that you most resent

Details of each set of values are provided below. In each case you are invited to identify the three value statements that matter most to you, a second group of three statements that come next in terms of importance and a final group of three that are next again in importance to you. The activity should help to bring home to you that other people may not share your priorities and that it is important for you to be aware of that if you hope to secure the commitment of others to your vision of a better future for your pupils.

Personal priorities (1): Reasons for becoming a teacher

Look at the list below of possible reasons for becoming a teacher.

Now individually identify what were, for you, the three most important reasons why you became a teacher, followed by a second group of three and then a final group of three. Include reasons not listed, if you wish.

(a) Family-friendly working hours and holidays (b) good salary (c)

desire to make a difference in children's lives (d) good pension (e) an opportunity to be professionally creative (f) sociable work context (g) good promotion prospects (h) job security (j) desire to give something back to society (h) some other reason – please specify

Find an opportunity to share your groupings with colleagues.

Prioritising Values (2): Characteristics of a good school

Look at the list below of characteristics of a good school.

Now individually identify what would be, for you, the three most important characteristics of a good school for your own children, followed by a second group of three and then a final group of three. Include characteristics not listed, if you wish.

Possible characteristics

(a) Accessibility (b) excellent home-school links (c) wide curricular choice (d) excellent leadership (f) excellent resources and accommodation (g) excellent teachers (h) the setting of high standards for all (i) excellent examination results (j) excellent specialist provision in music/art/drama (k) wide range of extra-curricular activities (l) minimal financial layout (n) some other factor – please specify

Find an opportunity to share your groupings with colleagues.

Prioritising Values (3): Desirable leadership attributes

Look at the list below of possible attributes of a good leader.

Now individually identify what would be, for you, the three qualities that you would most like others to attribute to you, followed by a second group of three and then a final group of three. Include attributes not listed, if you wish.

Possible attributes

(a) Optimism (b) courage (c) perseverance (d) integrity (e) ability to motivate (f) clear vision (g) open-mindedness (h) flexibility (i) team builder (j) transparency (k) puts children first (l) is a 'people person', (m) sense of humour (n) passion (o) some other attribute – please specify

Find an opportunity to share your groupings with colleagues.

Prioritising Values (4): Undesirable leadership attribute

Look at the list of leadership attributes below that you might resent in senior colleagues

Now individually identify what would be, for you, the three qualities that you would most resent in your senior colleagues, followed by a second group of three and then a final group of three. Include qualities not listed, if you wish.

Use the Diamond Pattern below to prioritise from the list of *possible* aspects of

Possible undesirable leadership attributes:

(a) Seldom praises – quick to blame; (b) does not listen; (c) indecisive; (d) criticises colleagues in public; (e) does not delegate; (f) manipulative; (g) autocratic;(h) divisive; (i) dwells on personal achievements; (j) treats colleagues as post holders and not people (k) some other aspect – please specify

Find an opportunity to share your groupings with colleagues

Activity WS2.4: Values Mapping

   (A)   Set out under the headings below the values you will bring to your role as a project leader

   (B)   Encapsulate those values in a brief vision or mission statement about what you hope to achieve as a project leader

A single example of each from a previous reader is provided to help you with your thinking.

Spiritual/Moral

I believe all pupils have been given talents that can be developed.

Social/Political

I believe good teaching can help any pupil overcome obstacles to learning

Leadership/Managerial

I believe in engaging my colleagues/pupils in the decision-making process as a means of motivating them

Vision/Mission Statement

There will be continuity, progression and coherence in the work that all pupils undertake in maths in the transition from P7 to S1.

Feedback: Activity WS2.1: School Cultures

Research indicates that there are several elements in the kind of school culture that is successful in times of change. Cultures that reflect a rather inflexible line management approach to change or the divisiveness of a balkanized set -up tend to be less effective than even the club culture, although such a culture is not likely to get the best out of all colleagues. Elements of the person culture are not unimportant and certainly the new professionalism in Scotland, post-McCrone, accepts that teachers should have a measure of autonomy, within the parameters of an agreed strategic vision and agreed aims.

The collaborative culture, however, is the culture most associated with successful schools and departments. At the heart of the collaborative culture is the involvement of all stakeholders in the future of the school. Staffs for their part are open to change and committed to seeing the best of changes being embedded in the way they go about things. It is interesting to note that recent (2010) interviews with the head teachers of two schools who received glowing reports from HMIE included constant references to working with pupils and parents, as well as teaching and support staff, towards developing a vision for the school and the involvement of everyone in achieving that vision. The relevance of Thought Piece 2.2 on a collegiate culture in all of this seems obvious.

Activity WS2.2: Mission and Aims

The best mission statements and aims are clear and purposeful assertions about what we stand for, about what we believe in, and about where we are going. They should spell out the kind of better future that the school perceives for itself and should be clear and comprehensible to a variety of audiences. They should also reflect the values that drive the school forwards. Such statements can inspire improvement.

It is important, however, to ensure that mission or vision statements are not mere pious platitudes. Vision statements should be reviewed at least annually. And leaders should lead discussion on the extent to which the statements reflect the reality of practice. They should encourage their team colleagues to justify and explain what they do in classrooms with reference to the underlying vision and values that they claim to endorse.

Below are two examples of a mission statement. The first one was composed after extensive consultation among staff, parents and pupils.

(a) Our Shared Vision – The School We Want To Be:

Ours is a learning community which has a 'can-do' ethos. It is a place where pupils, staff, parents and the wider community work together to make learning and teaching an enjoyable experience and where everyone involved is supported, challenged, engaged and motivated.

A group who were developing a policy on primary-secondary transition developed the second.

(b) We wish to ensure that every pupil will enter (secondary school) with enthusiasm, confident in the knowledge that all of his or her new teachers are committed to building on earlier learning to provide the best of educational experiences in a safe and happy environment.

Both mission statements might sound suitably pious and trite – but the important thing is that they were agreed in both cases by the staff in question. They were *their* mission statements!

Aims

Like the mission statement, aims should be drawn up in conjunction with the views of all and should be known by all. As with the mission statement, what is important is that those who are called upon to implement the aims should feel a commitment to them and, as always, the best way of securing commitment to achieving aims is to give people the chance to be involved in their formulation in the first place.

A departmental team in a school drew up the following aims and invited parents and pupils to comment before finalising them. They use them each year as a basis for auditing progress with regard to their achievement and for identifying priorities for improvement.

As a Department, our overall aim is to ensure that our pupils are secure, happy and successful academically and socially. To achieve this we shall:

1. *Make sure that our teaching and assessment methods for pupils exemplify best practice, including effective use of ICT*

2. *Develop programmes of study and teaching materials that provide challenging activities for pupils of all abilities*

3. *Provide pastoral, behavioural and learning support that matches the needs of pupils*
4. *Allocate resources and accommodation to agreed pupil priorities.*

5. *Work closely with parents and our other educational partners*

6. *Support staff development needs*

7. *Develop relevant quality assurance systems for the above*

Activity WS2.3: Prioritising values

(1) The desire to make a difference is almost always the main reason why people became teachers, followed by the desire to give something back in appreciation of a good education. The opportunity to be professionally creative is also usually high on the list. General job- satisfaction factors such as security, a sociable working environment and family-friendly hours find their place. The more 'selfish' reasons such as a good pension, salary or promotion prospects, while not unimportant, tend to come lower in the list than the others. And, generally, motives remain unchanged over the years. Such a finding says much for the altruism of teachers – a point we return to in *Session 3* on motivation.

(2) Teachers, like other parents, want schools where there are excellent teachers, excellent leadership and a climate that promotes high standards for all (In the latter connection there is often reference to the need for effective quality assurance systems) Excellent home-school links, examination results and wide curricular choice tend to come next. These are followed by excellent resources, the provision

of specialist subjects and the provision of extra-curricular activities. Issues of cost and accessibility tend to bring up the rear.

(3) Most leaders like to be seen as people who put children first. Highly rated attributes include the ability to inspire, usually by means of a clear and attractive vision. Integrity, open-mindedness and flexibility in achieving the vision are valued as is caring about people as individuals. Leaders themselves believe that it is important to retain a sense of humour and perspective. Optimistic perseverance is seen as a desirable quality, although it is important not to confuse perseverance with stubbornness, especially mis-placed stubbornness!

(4) Leaders who criticise in public and who have an autocratic desire to micromanage every detail while bullying folk into compliance are especially unpopular. Failure to listen or to provide colleagues with an opportunity to develop their own leadership skills is also strongly resented.

Judge for yourself the extent to which your own responses reflect the responses above. But do remember the need to take into account the values that are expressed by so many others if you are to have any success in securing the commitment of others to your ideals.

Activity WS2.4: Values mapping

Spiritual/Moral:

A range of religious, moral or ethical considerations drive most leaders but a common thread running through all of them tends to be a desire to promote mutual respect, equity and social justice

Social/Political:

Leaders, like teachers, want to have an impact on the lives of their pupils, wanting them to be all that they can be. They believe that schools can influence society and can reduce the impact of the various social factors that are known to place obstacles in the way of learning, rather than feeling helpless in the face of such factors.

Leadership/Managerial:

There is a firm commitment to participatory management and the consultative process although decisiveness on the part of the leader is also admired – even when decisions are not necessarily popular. There is a recognition that, given the diversity of attitudes and needs among the stakeholders of any school, it is impossible for any leader to please everyone. But decisions that are taken in all sincerity in the interests above all of pupils are likely to be respected.

Workshop Session 3: Motivating People and Building Teams

Workshop Session 3: Motivating People and Building Teams

Introduction

'No organisation can rely upon genius; the supply is always scarce and unreliable. It is the test of an organisation to make ordinary people perform better than they seem capable of, to bring out whatever strength there is in team members, and to use each person's strength to help all the other members perform.' (Drucker, P. 1988, *Management*: London: Pan Books, p 361)

Substitute 'team leader' for 'organisation' and Drucker's comments sum up perfectly the fundamental challenge for any leader. If leadership is about working with and through people in order to achieve objectives then it is clear that the ability to motivate others to give of their best is a key leadership skill, perhaps *the* key leadership skill. Little surprise that the *Standard for Team Leadership*, includes the ability to inspire and motivate others as individuals and as teams.

In this session we consider ways in which team leaders may motivate individual colleagues and try to identify the principles that may guide their efforts to get the best out of other people. We also look at how we may develop a team spirit among our colleagues in the belief that, as we noted earlier, none of us is as good as all of us.

Learning Outcomes

By the end of this workshop session readers will have:

- ✓ Read over thought pieces on motivation and team-building
- ✓ Reflected on key factors in motivating individual colleagues
- ✓ Recognised the importance of adapting leadership style to context
- ✓ Listed principles of motivation that they agree with
- ✓ Reflected on the qualities and skills required to build a team
- ✓ Reflected on the importance of well-managed meetings

Workshop Session 3: Motivating People and Building Teams

Thought Piece 3.1: Needs and motivation

N.B: The thought pieces for this session have been selected for their relevance to the motivation of professional individuals and teams.

They particularly reflect the importance of flexibility of approach on the part of the leader in cases where individualism may be quite strong.

The vast majority of teachers, if not indeed all teachers, come into the profession for altruistic reasons. They wish to make a difference in the lives of their pupils and to pay something back to society. For them the key word is service. Of course, they appreciate a decent salary and pension and job security. And of course the family-friendly working hours and holidays are a boon. But time and time again, teachers will tell you about the tremendous satisfaction they get simply from helping their pupils to be all they can be.

Yet in almost every school it is possible to find teachers who have become very cynical and who have long lost the drive and enthusiasm that characterised their early years in the profession. Sometimes they are worn down by work or family pressures and find it increasingly difficult to cope with the demands of the profession; sometimes they become bitter because they feel they have been unfairly passed over for promotion.

But sometimes the fault lies at the feet of senior management, both in terms of the systems, policies and procedures adopted by some school managers and also because of certain management styles. Indeed, research on behalf of Harvard Business School *("Stop De-motivating Your Employees!" Harvard Management Update, Vol. 11, No. 1, January 2006)* suggested that morale declined over time because of poor management practices in as many as 85% of companies. Too many, it seems, forget the needs of their colleagues.

Fundamental requirements

The research suggested that there are three fundamental needs that managers should take into consideration if they wish to get the best out of their colleagues, not just in the early years of their careers but in a continuing way over their entire careers:

Achievement

Teachers take a great pride in a good job well done and appreciate some *recognition* of their efforts to serve the needs of their pupils.

Equity

Teachers, like children, have a strong sense of *justice* and *fairness.*

They wish to be treated fairly in all aspects of their job and they strongly resent what they see as a lack of fairness.

Camaraderie

As with any other person, teachers have a great need to belong and so they value *productive relationships* with their colleagues.

Motivating people is ultimately about meeting their needs so all three of these requirements must be addressed if managers wish to get the best out of their colleagues. Lack of fairness cannot fully be compensated for by improved recognition. Recognition of individual performance will not fully compensate for poor relationships. And good relationships will be undermined if there is a lack of fairness of treatment.

If managers wish to help their colleagues to retain their initial enthusiasm they need to give due emphasis to the following eight practices, all of which are linked to the three fundamental requirements outline above:

Achievement – related

1. **Providing a raison d'etre**: a reason for being here! The idea of a vision or mission statement does not always get a good press and indeed if such a vision statement is simply constructed by one person and distributed among participating colleagues, it is likely to be greeted with loud groans and lip service at best.

   But when a leader sits down with his or her team to draw up a clear and credible overriding purpose for the work that they do there is a much greater chance that people will then work with increased enthusiasm to achieve that purpose. This is especially so if the leader goes on to explain how even the most mundane of tasks can contribute to the achievement of the overall vision.

   The story goes that President John F. Kennedy visited NASA some years after his famous declaration in 1961 that America would put a man on the moon by the end of the decade. Having spoken to a range of boffins, he then toured the facility and stopped off in an office to ask a young clerical assistant what she was doing. Oh, she said, I'm helping to put a man on the moon! Ask the man who sweeps up the debris at the end of the day at Disneyland in Florida what

78

he is doing and he will tell you that he is helping to bring happiness into the lives of children. In both organisations leaders had ensured that the contribution of everyone to achieving objectives was celebrated.

2. **Providing recognition**. It is remarkable the numbers of leaders who never seem to think of saying please or thank you but who are quick to criticise. Receiving personal recognition for the work you are doing is one of the most fundamental human needs. Yes, of course, people are paid for their work – even quite handsomely paid in some cases – but time and time again research makes it clear that mere money is not all that great a motivator. Leaders in education tend not to have powers such as the power to promote, the power to raise salaries – or indeed the power of hire and fire. But they can give their colleagues a word or a little note of appreciation of a good job well done. The best leaders do their best to catch their colleagues doing well so that the sincerity and relevance of their compliments can be recognised. Other leaders seem to delight in catching their colleagues out so that they can criticise them. So which sort of leader are you?

3. **Being a servant leader**. It sounds like a contradiction in terms, does it not? Yet in the world of education, where there is a considerable range of expertise and a great many self- motivated individuals in any school, there is a strong argument for declaring that the true job of a leader is to facilitate the work of those for whom s/he is responsible. And that includes leaving lots of decisions to teachers about where the priorities lie. 'What do you think should be done here, and how may I support you?' is an excellent question for any leader to ask so-called subordinates. And if for any reason you are not in a position to provide the support requested, then explain why and assure your colleagues that you will continue to make representations on their behalf so that the necessary support may be provided at a later date. Yet all too often, people seem to think that leadership is all about command and control. Perhaps it is the nature of the profession. But the numbers of school leaders who treat adults like children – and children as being beneath contempt – is a worry. And then they wonder why folk have become demotivated!

4. **Provide a feedback sandwich**. Your colleagues deserve

to know how they are doing and yet many leaders do not know how to do this without offending or discouraging them, especially if there is a need for them to improve some aspect of their performance. There are, of course, many strong characters in education who like you to tell them how it is and who will accept criticism if they see it as fair and constructive but the tendency to be defensive in the face of criticism is stronger again in most people.

This is where the *'feedback sandwich'* comes in. The principles are simple enough. First make sure that your colleagues are made aware regularly of how pleased you are with the good work they are doing (see 3 above) It is easier for colleagues to accept suggestions for improvement if they know that their leader is basically pleased with their work and is simply looking for ways for them to build on their existing skills to become even better.

Then be specific about any improvements that you feel your colleague should be working on in terms of teaching methods, materials or whatever and explain how you can assist them. Try to make sure that you focus on aspects of performance and not on some perceived personality flaws.

Then point out again that the aim is to build on existing skills. And when, hopefully, performance does improve, be quick to provide appropriate praise. So the sequence is praise – criticise – praise, with the criticism, in the sense of constructive criticism, being the meat in the sandwich!

There can be a particular problem when you try to offer criticism, or praise for that matter, to someone about something you know nothing about, say teaching methods in a subject where you have no expertise. In such cases, it is better to get someone who knows and understands the nature of the situation to look at any issues.

Equity- related

5. **Communicate** to your colleagues what they need and want to know. And the best way to provide them with what they want and need to know is to ask them! People can feel quite frustrated if they are left out of the information loop. 'Nobody ever tells me anything' may sometimes be an exaggeration but when someone is not informed about something that is going on then is easy for that person to feel that s/he is being

overlooked and is of no importance. Communicate regularly and communicate precisely. And make sure that you do what the communication promises will be done. Otherwise, before long, people will not trust your communications. Take care also to ensure that communications have been fully understood. Remember: meaning depends on what the receiver hears rather than what the transmitter sends. Full and meaningful communication not only helps your colleagues to do their jobs but indicates to them that they have your respect. A lack of communication may be perceived as a lack of respect.

6. **Deal with poor performance**. Poor performance does not only have an impact on the educational development of pupils. It can have an impact on the motivation and morale of other team members. Make sure that poor performers can have access to appropriate CPD and be prepared, if necessary, to take disciplinary action. Colleagues will expect you to deal with poor performance in a suitably professional way; they may well be de-motivated if the poor performer is seen to be 'getting away with it'. See more on this topic in *Session 3*.

Camaraderie-related

7. **Encourage teamwork.** In some ways, teamwork is not part of much of the job of teachers. Most of their days are spent within their classrooms working alone with their pupils. Indeed there are many teachers who are not even comfortable working with another adult. Yet there are clear benefits in gathering colleagues together to plan and implement a new approach, the use of new materials, better ways of assessing pupil work – whatever. This applies to gathering the people within a department; but it also applies to depute head teachers gathering people from across departments.

For one thing, it is very motivating for individual teachers to be invited to share in defining their role and its objectives. As we noted earlier, there is always a much greater chance of teachers being committed to implementing a plan or policy if they were involved in its formulation in the first place. And the benefits of peer coaching as people seek to overtake their shared objectives are becoming increasingly recognised. The desire to belong is as strong in teachers as it is in other people. That is why inviting colleagues to play a role in a team or working group is such an important means of motivating people.

Related to all three factors

8. **Listen and involve**. Teachers are a rich source of information about how to do a job and how to do it better. That is why participatory managers reap enormous benefits in terms of motivated colleagues and successful outcomes. They are forever inviting their colleagues to make suggestions on how to improve things. And they make sure that colleagues receive due recognition when suggestions are followed through and make a difference. They create an atmosphere where 'good enough' is not good enough and where proposals for improvement are welcomed.

Participatory managers also make sure that colleagues are free to use their own judgment commensurate with their knowledge and experience within agreed parameters. It is an interesting irony that the McCrone report, *A Teaching Profession for the 21st Century*, grew partially out of a demand for school managers to have their rights to manage clarified. Yet the underlying message of the report is the need to re-professionalise the profession in the sense of trusting individual teachers to behave in a professional manner. There are those who will let the side down. For the majority there is no single means of motivating teachers that is more powerful than allowing competent people to do their job as they see fit.

The research described above was carried out in industrial settings but school leaders can also de-motivate their colleagues. In a survey of leadership in primary schools some years ago, Christopher Day and his colleagues identified the following list of ten factors that were consistently a turn –off for people:

1 People are simply told that 'they must...'

2. People are put into a threatened position

3. Activities and responsibilities are not well- planned

4. It is felt that the plan is a 'gimmick' promoted by a senior member of staff to further his or her own ends

5. People feel that the plan is mounted merely to satisfy a higher authority

6. A lot of hard work is involved without any apparent or obvious results

7. Initial moves are badly organised, with consequential initial feed-back

8. People feel alienated from whoever is responsible for the plan

9. The team leader assumes the role of expert and there is a lack of opportunity for teachers to develop, or exercise, responsibility

10. There is group pressure from colleagues to 'opt out'

No 8, the point about alienation is particularly relevant. As was noted earlier, you are going to find it difficult to engage the commitment of anyone whom you alienate or who feels alienated from you. And the best way to find out is to ask them to state their position and to offer to explore the issues and 'clear the air' if possible.

Clearly, there is a variety of ways then in which a leader might contribute to or diminish the intrinsic motivation of his or her colleagues through the relationships that they establish. In the last analysis, however, after we have done what we can to create the kind of relationships within which there is the best chance of securing the commitment of colleagues towards the achievement of some objective, we must acknowledge that individuals themselves will ultimately decide whether, and to what extent, they want to become involved. And there are always a few mavericks or 'loose cannons' who seem to thrive on being perverse. There may also be a few 'burnt out cases' who seem to have lost all interest let alone enthusiasm for their jobs.

In such cases there is little option but to settle for compliance if not enthusiastic engagement. Leaders will rightly insist that their colleagues must at least carry out their duties and agreed policies in a basically competent manner while providing the essential resources for so doing. As a last resort, where performance is unacceptable and teachers are seriously disengaged despite all offers of support and encouragement, then it may be that the disciplinary process rather than the motivational process will have to take over. The vast majority, however, want to belong, want to contribute and, even when they are 'self-starters', appreciate being valued.

Implications for Team Leaders

What then are the practical steps for a leader trying to secure the commitment of others in planning and implementing some school improvement project? I would suggest they include the following:

- We should first be ready to make clear to our colleagues our own level of commitment to the project in focus and our hopes for what it may achieve for our pupils. People appreciate it if you make it clear to them where you are coming from − especially if, over time, you consistently match your actions to your declared values. Such behaviour on your part is an important first step in securing the respect of others.

- Then make it clear to others how much you value them. Spell out to others the kind of expertise that you know they have in terms of knowledge, skills and general commitment and make it clear how much you would appreciate it if they would contribute that expertise and commitment to the project. Emphasise appropriate aspects of their professional competence, not how nice they are. Flattery is worse than useless.

- In connection with this, explain to them precisely the role that you would like them to play in formulating and implementing any plans. People appreciate due recognition of their skills but also like to know where they stand. So they are inclined to be well-disposed to those who not only value them for their skills but also make clear what is wanted of them in terms of using those skills.

- The next step is to invite colleagues to make clear to you their own level of commitment and concern about the initiative. Inviting people to declare their position, and then respecting that position whatever it may be, is an important element in the motivation process. It is a way of demonstrating that you respect their values. Spend some time on this step. Invite people to explain any reluctance they may have. Ask them directly if there is anything in the relationship that exists between you that is part of the problem and invite them to indicate what would change their attitudes. Try to persuade them to engage for at least a limited trial period with the promise of a review of any aspect of the situation about which they are not happy. Make it clear that their proposals will receive serious consideration. If they just do not wish to be involved then accept their decision and make it clear to them that you hold no grudges. But do not beg.

The steps that follow are based on the assumption that you do succeed in getting them at least to 'suck it and see'.

- Go on to set challenging but realistic goals in consultation with the colleagues who will be called upon to implement these goals. The work of *Albert Bandura* over the last thirty years on the concept of *self-efficacy* is important here. Self-efficacy is essentially the belief that a person has that he or she has the ability to plan and undertake a given course of action. It plays a key role in motivation as people will tend to regulate the amount of effort they put into something in accordance with the impact they expect their actions to have and the importance they attach to such impact. In simple terms, people are more inclined to take on a task if they believe that they can succeed and if the degree of challenge interests them enough. Involving colleagues in setting goals is therefore an important means of securing their commitment to achieving them.

- Make sure you provide the tools for the job in the shape of CPD, suitable accommodation and materials – and time. Self-efficacy is again relevant here. A person's confidence in their own abilities with regard to any particular task will certainly be influenced by the availability or otherwise of appropriate resources and support. If promised resources are not forthcoming, then action plans will need to be adjusted accordingly.

- Continue to provide colleagues with feedback that is specific, constructive and relevant to what they have been doing. Remember that they will be simultaneously evaluating their own efforts so avoid flattery and patronising comments that they will have no difficulty in seeing through. Even negative feedback is positive when the recipient recognises it as constructive.

- Invite your colleagues to participate in evaluating the impact of your joint efforts. Success, and the recognition of success, is a great way of maintaining motivation over time, especially when colleagues are involved in shaping goals in the first place. And such involvement will make them more willing to re-adjust if required.

85

Thought Piece 3.2: (a) Power and Motivation

Our ways of motivating people are closely linked to our perceptions of the nature and sources of power and to our preferred styles of leadership. As leaders, we derive our power from one or more of the following sources:

(a) Position power: One obvious source of power is the position held. As a promoted person, you have a certain amount of legitimate power that is vested in the position you hold within the hierarchy. You have a right to take certain decisions and you will certainly be held accountable for the use of the power delegated to you.

(b) Personality power: This is the kind of power whereby leaders may influence their colleagues by sheer force of personality. Sometimes described as charismatic power, this is the kind of power that is often found in people from a very young age. It may have nothing to do with the actual position that a person holds in the hierarchy. The power may exist even although the person exhibiting it has their own flaws.

(c) Expert power: Expert power derives from the special knowledge or skills that the leader may have in relation to the subject that is being taught. It may also be derived from the ability to recognise and make use of expertise in others, including quite junior members of a team

(d) Reward power: This power derives from the ability of the leader to provide rewards. In teaching this may be in the shape of praising staff and making them feel valued by trusting them with certain duties, by ensuring that they are given appropriate support, by doing them the occasional favour and by pushing their claims for promotion.

(e) Coercive power:

This is the power to force someone to do something against their will and is often the power used by micro-managers, autocrats and bullies. Other forms of power can also be used in coercive ways, such as when a reward or expertise is withheld, personality power is used to threaten social exclusion or position power is used to insist that someone must do something or face the consequences.

Thought Piece 3.2 (b): Emotional Intelligence, Leadership Style and Motivation

The work of Daniel Goleman over the last twenty years has done much to raise our awareness of emotional intelligence and its relevance to leadership, including school leadership.

As the name implies, emotional intelligence is concerned with knowing and understanding feelings, as opposed to facts or concepts. More specifically, it is the ability that each of us has in varying degrees:

- ✓ to know and understand our own feelings and to be confident about managing them, even in challenging situations
- ✓ to be sensitive to the feelings of others and to be influential in helping others to manage their feelings.

Described thus, it is not difficult to see why leaders need to have high levels of emotional intelligence. And ideally leaders will have the ability to call upon a balanced combination of the two broad sets of skills. Yet many leaders tend to favour one dimension over the other.

Self –awareness and self-management

We can all think of leaders who exibit very high levels of self-confidence. They demonstrate a personal drive to achieve, initiative and self-control. They are personally very conscientious and are likely to demonstrate high levels of personal integrity and comptence. They are the kind of people who tend to fit the description of 'workaholic'. They often expect others to be workaholics too.

On the downside, such leaders may be quite insensitive to the needs of others. They can be quite inflexible and tend towards micro-management, insisting upon control over every detail in a situation.

For such leaders, it sometimes seems that results are all that matters, no matter the consequences for other people. As a consequence they run the risk of de-motivating others.

Awareness and management of others

We have all met leaders whom we would describe as 'people persons'. The chances are that we would like to describe ourselves in that way. Such leaders have a marked empathy for the needs of others. Indeed such leaders would subscribe to the notion of leadership as a form of service to one's colleagues.

They have a particular skill in recognising, harnessing and developing the skills of others, their listening skills are highly developed and they are skilled in managing conflict in a productive way. They are also skilled in building teams

On the downside, they run the risk sometimes of consulting so extensively that they never quite get round to taking decisions. They may lack strength in their own convictions and tend to be guided by 'pooled ignorance'. Above all, they may tend to make excuses for the incompetence of some people and fail to 'grasp the nettle' when results are poor.

Research by consultants Hay McBer[1] on almost 4000 company executives across the world refined the broad leadership dimensions described above into six leadership styles, each originating from different aspects of emotional intelligence and each having implications for the climate or culture of an organisation.

1. The Coercive Leader
The coercive leader proceeds essentially by issuing instructions. Unquestioning obedience to these instructions is expected. Such a style might be appropriate in the early stages of training employees who lack knowledge, skill or experience. But it is the least effective style in most normal situations for creating a learning climate, not least because it is so inflexible and uncompromising. It is unlikely to be appropriate in a school setting, other than during a fire drill or in connection with some other safety issue.

2. The Pace-Setting Leader
The pace-setting leader sets high personal performance standards and expects others to meet them also. The pace-setter expects employees to follow his or her example rather than to show personal initiative. There tends to be a lack of delegation. The result is that the pace-setting style can destroy a positive work environment, as employees feel they will never be good enough and their morale falls. On the other hand, the pace-setter is not willing to tolerate incompetence or poor results. Poor employees are expected to 'shape up or ship out'.

1 Hay Worldwide at: www.haygroup.com/

3. The Affiliative Leader

The affiliative leader believes 'people come first' and consequently tries to create harmony by building strong emotional bonds. The approach will improve communication and, as people begin to share ideas this will increase inspiration and a shared purpose. Flexibility will also be improved as people are given the freedom to do their jobs in the way which they think is most effective. It is particularly helpful when trying to build harmony, increase morale, improve communication or repair a breakdown in trust. On the downside, the affiliative leader may avoid taking an approach to dealing with poor performance that is hard edged enough. Decisiveness and giving a clear lead may also suffer.

4. The Democratic Leader

This approach has much in common with the affiliative style and by giving other people a share in the decision-making process it promotes a sense of ownership, trust and commitment and high morale. It works well in schools as teachers bring a range of knowledge, skills and talents to the service. It is less appropriate, however, in situations where the decision has already been taken and the emphasis is on pushing forward in the early stages of trying to deal with some critical situation.

5. The Authoritative Leader

As the title suggests, the authoritative leader demonstrates personal knowledge and wisdom of a kind that attracts the respect of followers in a way that mere position does not. As a visionary, the authoritative leader is able to maximise commitment to the organisation's goals and strategy. The research indicated that the authoritative style is probably the most effective, having a positive impact on all environmental factors, although it works less well with a team of experts or peers who are themselves authoritative.

6. The Coaching Leader

Coaching leaders help employees to identify their strengths and weaknesses and link them to career goals. They also encourage employees to develop a personal development plan. As good delegators, they give employees challenging assignments. The style works less well with employees who are resistant to change or where the leader lacks the quite sophisticated coaching skills that are required – and it tends to be the style least used

The first two of these leadership styles relate to those leaders who are strong on self-management and less strong in managing others. The remaining four all include strong elements of the kind of empathy that is required to manage other people.

Conclusion

The study came up with the following conclusions:
- Leaders who have mastered four or more styles, especially authoritative, democratic, affiliative and coaching, have both the best work environment and outstanding business performance.

- The most effective leaders switch flexibly among styles
- Leaders who used styles that positively affected the work environment had better financial results than those who did not. The authoritative style had the most positive overall impact, followed by the affiliative, democratic and coaching styles Pace-setting and coercive styles have a negative impact.

These descriptions are caricatures to a certain extent and it seems likely that every leader has elements of all styles, with even the most empathetic and democratic of leaders being quite autocratic on occasion. But the overall finding about the effectiveness of leaders who are able to adapt styles to a given situation is very important.

The original findings were based on a study of business executives but interestingly similar research into headship on behalf of the Ministry of Education in England in 2000 indicated that the best academic results were to be found in schools where leaders exhibited four or more management styles.

Unsurprisingly, the successful styles were once again the authoritative, the affiliative, the democratic and the coaching style. There will always be times when a leader may have to insist upon a certain course of action but the research suggested that leaders who were persistently autocratic and prone to micromanagement alienated and de-motivated colleagues – and pupil attainment suffered accordingly.

Thought Piece 3.2 (c): Nine ways of influencing others

Just as they use different types of power, leaders also use different ways of *influencing* people. Leaders with no formal access to power may nevertheless use the same techniques. The lists below summarises the commonest ways of influencing people.

Influencing others

Rational persuasion: The person uses logical arguments and factual evidence to persuade you of the viability and desirability of a proposal

Inspirational appeal: The person arouses your enthusiasm by appealing to your values, ideals and aspirations

Consultation: The person seeks your participation in planning a strategy that you will be called upon to implement

Ingratiation: The person flatters you or otherwise seeks to make you feel favourable towards them before asking you to do something

Exchange: The person offers you an exchange of favours if you help to accomplish the task

Personal appeal: The person appeals to your feelings of loyalty and friendship towards them before asking you to do something

Coalition: The person seeks the assistance of others to persuade you to do something

Legitimation: The person claims the right or authority to make a request on the basis of their position in a hierarchy

Pressure: The person uses demands, threats or persistent reminders to influence you to do what they want

Power– Influence Combinations to motivate people

The autocratic combination:

This combines coercive and legitimate power with pressure, coalition and legitimation tactics. Even if expert or personality power is used, the overall purpose is still domination.

The carrot and stick combination:

This combines the use of legitimate, coercive or reward power with exchange and to a certain extent pressure tactics

The transformational combination:
This combines expert and personality power with such influence approaches as consultation, inspirational appeal and rational persuasion.

Thought Piece 3.3: The drivers of motivation

In his book, '*The Motivated School*', Alan McLean explains how teachers may motivate pupils by means of four 'drivers':

Engagement is how teachers show they are interested in and value pupils

Structure refers to the clarity of goals and the pathways towards them whereby teachers let pupils know what is expected of them

Stimulation comes from a curriculum that is interesting to the pupil and that sets challenging but achievable targets for them

Feedback lets pupils know how they are doing and, properly used, is one of the strongest motivational tools the teacher can use

McLean points out that 'child-centred teaching needs teacher-centred management, and management at all levels need to treat teachers the same way they expect teachers to treat their students.' Thus:

Engagement is how leaders show they are interested in and value staff

Structure refers to the clarity of goals and the pathways towards them whereby leaders let staff know what is expected of them

Stimulation comes from a range of tasks that are interesting to staff and that set challenging but achievable targets for them

Feedback lets staff know how they are doing and, properly used, is one of the strongest motivational tools the leader can use.

McLean also points out an important link between leadership and management style and motives for seeking leadership in the first place:

'All of us are highly motivated to exercise control over our lives. Some people are keen to control others. Such people often appear similar to those with positive self-esteem in that they feel capable and optimistic. They will probably have had positive experiences of exercising control over important life events that will have helped to contribute to their feelings of competency. On the other hand, for others, exercising control may be a way of maintaining fragile self-esteem. They fight their feelings by striving to control other aspects of their lives.

Some people with a high desire for control will satisfy this need through leadership positions. The management style of such people will be a function of how their desire for control has developed through their lives. Those whose leadership drive is based on a healthy self-esteem show confidence trust and respect in their working relationships.

In contrast, those whose desire for control is driven by fragile self-esteem may have a tendency to be over –dominant, rigid or manipulative in their relationships with colleagues. Difficulty with trusting people combined by a desire for control may not be all that uncommon. Those attracted to leadership to meet their own needs allow their needs to take priority over everyone else's needs. The enhancement of their personal status becomes their guiding principle. Their interactions with others are geared to achieving their own agenda rather than supporting teachers to meet their own particular and group goals. They need to be centre stage and cannot put their ego to one side long enough to work for the common cause.'

McLean, A. (2004) (edited)

Leaders who are secure in their own worth, including an ability to recognise their shortcomings, have little difficulty in delegating and encouraging others to take decisions. They understand the paradox of power – the more you share power, the more powerful you become.

But leaders who are masking their fragile self-esteem or who are fundamentally insecure are more likely to adopt a control and command style. As we have noted elsewhere, such a style is not appropriate in modern society and certainly not in schools where teachers have a due sense of their own worth. Readers might wish to reflect upon whether their own leadership drives come from a healthy or a fragile self-esteem.

Thought Piece 3.4: Leading and Building Teams

Introduction

Teamwork, a collegial approach and effective use of collegial time in order to promote effective learning and teaching are recognised as potentially powerful motivators. Yet the teaching profession, of its very nature, more often than not relies upon the work of individual teachers in classrooms. Indeed, as has been noted in another extract, one of the great challenges of leadership in schools is to find the right balance between attending to the needs of the institution on the one hand and the needs of the individual teacher on the other.

Research into effective and ineffective departments in secondary schools indicates that team leaders themselves are of the view that a team approach to delivering the education provision for which they are responsible is an essential component in motivating individual members of the team to achieve results and that departments that lack a team spirit are less effective.

In primary schools, where the 'team' might be the whole staff there are similar indications that the staff team can achieve more by working together than they could by working individually. This is understandable. A desire to belong is strong in most of us and any teacher who has worked in a collegial climate of mutual respect and in a situation where there are poor inter-personal relationships will readily attest to the fact that it is much more difficult to give of one's best in a tense and divisive context.

A leader who is able to harness the range of skills that is likely to be available among team members before channelling them in the required direction is likely to be more effective than someone who is perhaps barely aware even of the talents that his or her colleagues may have. Of particular importance is the ability of the leader to promote the kind of team ethos in which individual teachers care about each other as well as their pupils and are willing to support each other in their work.

A team approach is particularly important in developing the plans, policies and procedures by which teaching and learning will be delivered. Team members will be much more inclined to commit themselves to the implementation of a particular approach if they have been jointly involved in its formulation in the first place. And from the pupil perspective, there will be a consistency and coherence of approach that will enhance their learning.

Individual teachers will always bring their own personalities to the learning and teaching process but there is enough information about the characteristics of effective learning and teaching to know that as pupils progress through and across the curriculum there should be a certain consistency of approach.

Teams or groups
It is important to distinguish between these terms. A group may be quite a loose gathering of people and indeed at the first meeting of your own group, this might be the very word to describe them!

A team, however, suggests a group of people working together on the basis of shared perceptions, agreed aims and objectives and a commitment to work with one another in the belief that together the members can achieve more by sharing their expertise than could be achieved by any of them individually.

Stages in Team Building

Researchers have identified four stages in the process of teambuilding. The four stages seem particularly relevant to a situation where a team leader is trying to establish a working party to work on a school-based improvement project.

Stage 1: Forming:

This is most obvious in a newly created group where folk are getting the measure of each other and there is tentativeness about who fits in where. In an established team the same stage is likely to be exhibited where the team is facing a new challenge, one perhaps that is different from the usual challenges that they have faced before, or when a new member joins. Characteristics of this stage include hesitancy about sharing feelings and about making innovative suggestions and a conformity to the status quo. There is more talk than listening, little shared understanding and leaders at odds with their followers.

Stage 2: Storming:

At this stage a team decides that it wants to review its operating methods in an effort to improve its performance. People begin to open up, perhaps saying things that they have wanted to say for years. There may be conflict as proposals for new approaches and who does what are generated and debated. There may be a degree of discomfort and insecurity as some home truths are expressed. Some people might even want to disengage. But overall there is a new openness and a new willingness to listen and to think as a first step to operating in a more unified way.

Stage 3: Norming:

Gradually the team begins to resolve the interpersonal issues that feature so strongly at stage 2 and begins to devise or revise its ground rules. The status quo of Stage 1 may well be revisited but this time everyone has apart in framing purposes, methods of working and quality assurance arrangements. People are persuaded to give their commitment, for a trial period at the very least, to initiatives. In an established team, it may be that there is some revision of roles and duties in relation to a new challenge or a new arrival

Stage 4: Performing:

The three previous stages have been successfully negotiated, people have settled into their roles and the team starts to be really effective in achieving its agreed purposes. Debate will continue but it will be constructive.

Thought Piece 3.5: Meetings and team-building

It is difficult, not to say impossible, to develop a performing team without having regular and well-organised meetings of the team. Meetings can be an extremely useful communications vehicle and clearly provide many opportunities for a consultative and collaborative approach to decision-making. They also provide excellent opportunities for the team leader to demonstrate leadership values-in-practice, to 'walk the talk' as it is often described. And the potential for using meetings to motivate reluctant colleagues, especially if there is a critical mass of support for a given proposal, is considerable.

Yet meetings, if not properly managed, can have a negative impact that diminishes goodwill and support and slows down the development of a performing team. So it is worth reflecting on the role of the chairperson and the possible consequences of that role for the effectiveness of meetings. We may identify five particularly important aspects of that role:

Climate setting

This includes all those aspects of the role of the chair that are concerned with setting the tone of meetings – from ensuring suitably comfortable surroundings to emphasising the value placed upon the views of members - and to establishing the rules of behaviour and setting a good example. Careful planning before the meeting will contribute to the tone of it – as will a sense of humour.

Leading the discussion

This includes such matters as focusing firmly on the agreed purpose of the meeting and related items, exercising authority, summarising discussions and being ready to open up new perspectives, especially where the team has perhaps become settled and comfortably complacent in its ways. It also involves seeing opportunities for inviting another team member to lead the discussion.

Gate-keeping

This is essentially concerned with taking the steps that will ensure that everyone has the opportunity to be heard. It may involve encouraging the quieter, less confident colleague to speak up or bringing in a less motivated colleague by encouraging the person to talk about some aspect of the discussion that does interest them. It is likely also to involve curtailing the power of the dominant, the rambler and the disruptive joker by insisting that all speak through the chair.

Refereeing

This involves keeping your head when all around are losing theirs! It may involve staying neutral in those situations where you are perfectly happy to accept any one of a number of options that are being debated. It is likely to involve calming conflict among team members while encouraging healthy debate. And it is about blowing the whistle for time up. Folk need to get away!

Administering

This is concerned with ensuring that agendas are drawn up and issued in advance; keeping to time, ensuring that a proper record of the meetings is kept and that 'next steps' are clearly identified. Sloppy administration, like a sloppy approach to the other roles, can seriously reduce the potential of a meeting as a teambuilding event.

Thought Piece 3.6: How not to influence people: A cautionary tale

There once was a woman called Barbara who was very ambitious and who wanted to go all the way ultimately to headship of a school. Barbara had many of the attributes of leadership. She was knowledgeable, experienced, competent and hard working. She succeeded in being promoted to head of a 6- member department in the school and there was no doubt that, at that level, her personal drive and subject expertise contributed much to the overall success of the department in terms at least of pupil attainment.

Barbara knew how good she was. Nothing much wrong with that! Her subject expertise and excellent teaching skills in particular stood her in good stead as head of her department. But unfortunately, she could not resist telling everyone how good she was – frequently. She would personally take all the high profile classes, especially those who were likely to do well in national examinations and she usually tried to do everything herself as she had no confidence that her colleagues could do things as well as she could. If anyone tried to suggest ideas to Barbara, she would either say yes I know and I am already doing that very well or would dismiss the ideas out of hand. Then she would order her colleagues around, sometimes while using their ideas.

Before long, Barbara began to apply for promotion to senior management team level, both within her own school and other schools in the area. But she was never successful. Time and time again it seemed to Barbara that colleagues whom she would not see in her way were passing her by.

She did ask for feedback but was usually palmed off with remarks that she had done well but it was just that others performed better on the day.

Eventually she approached a family friend who was a head teacher and asked him to explain as bluntly as possible why she was not succeeding in getting into senior management. The friend went on to explain that so long as she continued to antagonise colleagues with her know-all attitudes, her tendency to claim all the credit and her endless-self promotion then, without realising it, she was sending signals that she was a junior. And junior people do not become senior managers.

Barbara was coping with demands at her departmental level mainly because of her personal competence – though in truth the department would have been even more successful if she had given her colleagues a chance to shine every now and again. But she had no chance of succeeding at higher levels where it is just not possible to do everything and where the emphasis is even more on harnessing the talents around you and giving them direction.

If you feel the need constantly to be telling others how wonderful you are and to take all the credit for your achievements, then pretty soon others will stop giving you the credit you seek and come to the conclusion that ultimately you are insecure.

The trick to becoming a senior leader is to act as if you already are a senior leader. Do what the best senior leaders do *after* they are senior leaders, not what you think you need to do *to become* a senior leader. Once she understood that distinction, Barbara changed her strategy. She talked up other people, gave them more credit, and tried to get them promoted. She also changed her focus from her department to the whole school. Effective senior leaders don't prioritise their own departments over other areas; they think about what's good for the school as a whole and for children *across* the curriculum.

Rather than think of herself as an expert, Barbara began to look at the expertise that was available under her very nose. In the past, she had tried to do everything and seldom delegated. Now, she looked for opportunities for promotion for her colleagues so they would continue to grow. In the past she had spent most of her time advocating her own opinion, which she thought made her sound knowledgeable. Now she asked more questions and explored other people's perspectives, which made her seem wise and open. Over time, *acting* wise actually *made* her wise. She didn't just appear senior; she became senior. Today Barbara is a head teacher. But there are many 'Barbaras' around. Some of them are even men! And many of them might read a paper like this, nod their heads in sage agreement – and fail to realise that they fit the picture.

Thought Piece 3.7: An example of good practice

Some years ago a school was inspected and a certain team leader was commended for her efforts to build a team spirit and motivate her colleagues, even although there was a strong resistance to change among those colleagues. The inspector explained what was so impressive:

- ✓ Her own love of her subject and her desire to share it with children is exemplary

- ✓ Her approach to uncommitted staff is exactly the same as it is for more committed staff – except that she has to work much harder

- ✓ She accepts the reality of her situation – and the colleagues she has

- ✓ She has a very clear vision of what she wants to achieve - and articulates it all the time

- ✓ She constantly exemplifies her vision – she walks the talk

- ✓ She is sensitive to the needs of her colleagues as people and not just as post-holders

✓ She takes every opportunity to develop her staff – constantly demonstrating her methods in an effort to encourage them

✓ When they are resentful of change, she shows endless patience in explaining her ideas

✓ She involves them at every opportunity in discussions – and gives them the opportunity to lead the debate on relevant topics

✓ She invites them to lead specific projects, makes sure they have the necessary support and is quick to acknowledge their successes

✓ She seeks advice from the local authority about CPD opportunities and encourages her colleagues to undertake professional development

✓ When progress is slow, she resists the temptation to intervene and just do the thing herself

✓ She tackles difficult situations firmly but fairly

✓ When all else fails – she just tries and tries again.

This concludes the thought pieces for this workshop session.

Session 3: Workshop Activities

NB: The activities in this workshop are for aspiring middle and senior managers alike.

Activity WS3.1: Motivational drivers, Power, Influence and Style

Look at the five sources of power listed in *Thought Piece 3.2 (a)*, the six leadership styles listed in *Thought Piece 3.2 (b)* and the nine influencing tactics listed in *Thought Piece 3.2 (c)* Individually, identify an occasion when you were very successful in persuading someone to do something that they did not really want to do OR an occasion when you were unsuccessful.

Use the list of questions below (based on *Thought Piece 3.3*) to jot down briefly the key 'drivers', the key source of power, the influencing tactics and the leadership style that you used in the situation in question. What, on reflection, was the key to your success or failure in terms of the 'drivers', power source, influencing targets or style that you used? Share your experiences if possible.

Engagement: What did you do to show interest in and value of the person?

Structure: What did you to make requirements clear?

Stimulation: What did you do to interest the person in the challenge?

Feedback: What did you do to let the person know how they were doing?

Source of Power: Which source of power did you mainly rely upon?

Leadership Style: Which leadership style did you mainly rely upon?

Influencing tactic: Which influencing tactics did you mainly rely on?

Activity WS3.2: Team Building

Look again at *Thought Piece 3.4* and in particular the section that deals with the four stages of team building. Now think of any team of which you have been a member and which did not always reach the 'performing' stage.

(a) Individually complete the quality indicator overleaf *as it relates to the team in question.* Use the rating code below to assess the stage of *teambuilding* that the team has reached in *each* of the *seven* characteristics listed:

1 = forming 2 = storming 3 = norming 4 = performing

For example, you might allocate a 4 to a team where every member has clearly defined and fairly distributed duties but a 1 for distributed leadership if the leader of that same team seldom delegates.

(b) List the qualities and skills that *you* would need as a team leader to maximise your chances of turning the team into a performing team. You may find List 4 from the *Standard for Team Leadership* useful (It is repeated after the Quality Indicator on teamwork)

(c) Now look again at *Thought Piece 3.1* List the intrinsic needs of the *members of the team* (in no particular order) that would probably need to be addressed before the 'performing' stage of aspect *No 1: Demonstrate commitment to a common purpose* could be achieved. Use the needs analysis form that follows List 4 to identify the key needs that the team members in question are likely to have – not necessarily as many as eight!

(d) Now jot down any potential consequences for *pupils* if the team continued not to reach the 'performing' stage of aspect No 1.

Quality Indicator: Teamwork

How are you doing?   **How do you know?**

As a team you:	Illustrations: As a team you have:	Rating
1. Demonstrate commitment to a common purpose	A clearly defined shared vision; agreed aims and objectives; a commitment to work together; agreed action plans	
2. Operate in a climate of trust	An atmosphere in which members respect each other; a belief that all want the best; an atmosphere of enthusiasm	
3. Have clear job specifications	A fair distribution of duties; responsibility for clearly defined areas; clear targets	
4. Have distributed leadership	Individual opportunities to lead a given aspect of an initiative; opportunities to contribute particular expertise; agreement about how final decisions shall be made	
5. Participate and cooperate	Everyone involved in discussions; a shared perception of being involved in meaningful consultation; a readiness to listen to each other; conflict dealt with in a productive way; readiness to work with other team	
6. Communicate openly	Confidence to say what you want to say; a lack of private agendas; a lack of "baggage"; transparency in debate	
7. Review team effectiveness	Assess your team strengths and areas for improvement on a regular basis; invite others to comment on your effectiveness; seek improvement in order to keep on performing as a team	

List 4: Personal Qualities and Interpersonal Skills: A Team Leader:

- ✓ Understands and can control personal emotions
- ✓ Understands and can help others control their emotions
- ✓ Creates and maintains a positive atmosphere and team spirit
- ✓ Takes account of the values and views of others, including parents, children and young people
- ✓ Inspires and motivates others
- ✓ Thinks strategically within the relevant area of responsibility
- ✓ Uses effective decision-making processes and problem-solving techniques
- ✓ Communicates effectively in terms both of providing information and inviting and listening to feedback

Needs Analysis: List the needs of *team members* that may have to be addressed if the leader is to promote a common purpose

1.

2.

3.

4.

5.

6.

7.

8

Chairing Meetings: Introduction

It is difficult, if not impossible, to build a performing team without having regular meetings of team members. But it is essential for these meetings to be well organised and well-led if the time allocated to them is to be wisely used. The role of the chair or team leaders in this regard is clearly vital and it is to this important function that we now turn.

Activity WS 3.3: Chairing Meetings

Look again at *Thought Piece 3.5: Meetings and teambuilding*

List under the following headings the most common failings by the chairperson in terms of:

- Climate setting:

- Leading the discussion:

- Gate-keeping:

- Refereeing:

- Administering:

What were the consequences for the value of the meeting of these failings?

Feedback: Activity WS3.1: Motivational drivers, Power, Influence and Style
As should be clear from the cases discussed in plenary, one of the key marks of an excellent team leader is to be able to identify the essential elements in any situation and then adopt the relevant

leadership style rather than sticking always with the one style. It is important in this connection for the leader to recognise the needs of the individual team member, the needs of the situation and the needs of the leader as well. It may well be that a young teacher is happy to receive clear guidance and instructions about what is to be done and how. The same might apply for that matter to an experienced teacher who is happy to leave all the new planning and organising to the leader.

But it can be extremely de-motivating for a confident, competent and self-motivated teacher to be told what to do instead of being trusted to get on with things. Yet research indicates that most leaders stick with one leadership style no matter what the situation and that as few as 1% of leaders can move comfortably among the full range of styles.

As was noted in *Thought Piece 3.2 (b),* research into headship on behalf of the Ministry of Education in England in 2000 indicated that the best academic results were to be found in schools where leaders exhibited four or more management styles. There will always be times when a leader has to insist upon a certain course of action but the research suggested that leaders who were persistently autocratic and prone to micromanagement alienated and de-motivated colleagues – and pupil attainment suffered accordingly.

Feedback: Activity WS3.2 (a): Team Building

(a) Ratings with regard to stages of team building in each of the seven characteristics will obviously vary according to individual responses.

(b) The steps you take to develop a performing team will involve your calling upon *all* of the elements of professional skills and abilities that are listed in *Table 4* – and calling upon them again and again. In particular you will need to make clear your own commitment to the project in hand and be ready to lead an open discussion about the attitudes of those who are to work with you. Any conflicting views should be tackled head on and should be seen as an opportunity for clarifying issues and seeking potentially more effective ways of proceeding with the project. In all of this, you should be consistently emphasising the inter-dependence of the members of the team if success is to be achieved. You must, of course, maintain clarity of focus and a determination to proceed on an agreed basis. If agreement just cannot be reached over a given issue then you must decide which line is to be followed, inviting your colleagues to support the proposed line at least on a trial basis subject to further review. Personal perseverance is extremely important in seeking the commitment of others.

If all else fails and a team member simply is not willing to engage in teamwork, quite possibly for reasons that have nothing to do with the needs of pupils, then you may have to insist and instruct. This is a last resort, however. The imposition of a team approach can never be as powerful as the embracing of team approach.

Quite often the task of the team leader will be to motivate colleagues to overtake goals that have been set externally by senior colleagues or by central authorities. In these cases, a style that is supportive in trying to make sure that colleagues at least have the necessary time and resources to achieve these goals will be of particular importance. It is worth realising too that meeting external targets does not preclude ownership of the starting point (See further in *Session 5*)

(c) In education, *intrinsic motivation*, where the desire to perform is triggered by meeting the individual's *internal needs,* is much more effective and sustainable than *extrinsic* motivation, where the pressure to perform comes from outside the person. So identifying and addressing the intrinsic needs of your colleagues is always a good idea if you are to have the best chance of persuading them to give of their best, both as individuals and as team members.

In terms of team-building, there is always the possibility that in addressing the different needs of different people you may have to prioritise. But you will not lose good will overall so long as you are ready to explain your decisions and so long as you make sure that all priorities are addressed at some time or another.

In general terms, the following needs are among the most common that must be addressed in order to sustain and build intrinsic motivation and to promote a common purpose among the team.

> Significance: the need for one's job and oneself to be valued
> Identity: the need to see how one's work contributes to team goals
> Responsibility
> Respect
> Recognition
> Feedback
> Intellectual stimulation
> Organisational justice and fairness

(d)   There is considerable potential for confusion among pupils if their teachers do not work towards an agreed vision, aims and approaches. Teachers in secondary school departments for example can confuse pupils if they go their own way – especially if their way is different from a teacher in the same department who took the pupils the previous year. The same applies in primary schools. Some years ago, an initiative that involved following pupils for a day or so across the curriculum revealed the serious inconsistencies that pupils were exposed to, not only in teaching methods but also in assessment standards. There was no doubt that pupil learning was being affected, often by teachers unwittingly undermining the efforts of each other to raise standards by contradictory demands. This confusion also extended across departments with, for example, teachers in the physics department in a school providing pupils with problems that they could not solve as the mathematics department in the same school had yet to deal with the mathematical processes that were necessary to solve the physics problems.

Feedback: Activity WS3.3: Chairing meetings

Unfortunately it is quite possible that you have attended – or even led - several meetings that were wasteful of time. The list below is based on the work of Everard and Morris (2004) who have identified a number of common faults in poorly conducted meetings, all of which contributed to an overall feeling of poor management:

➢ Lack of a clear overall purpose
➢ No agenda or too large an agenda
➢ Emphasis on information-giving rather than consultation
➢ Failure to invite members to contribute to or chair a meeting
➢ No record of previous decisions
➢ Failure to issue relevant papers in advance
➢ Lack of proper pacing
➢ One person (including the chair) doing all the talking
➢ Poor allocation of time
➢ No minute keeping or any record of agreed next steps

Their findings related to general staff meetings but many of them are equally relevant to the meetings of ad hoc working groups or established teams. As you undertake an initiative, it is likely that you will have a reservoir of goodwill at your disposal. But over time, your scope for calling meetings and then chairing them effectively will have a considerable impact on the team spirit that you are able to generate and maintain - a spirit that in its turn is such a major factor in producing performing teams.

Successful meetings, whether one-to-one or in groups, invariably feature excellent listening skills on the part of the team leader. Many researchers believe that listening carefully is even more important than speaking clearly and emphasise the importance of a number of principles, listed below, that are fundamental for developing such listening skills:

• Concentrating on the speaker and relevant body language
• Demonstrating that you are listening by appropriate sounds and nods
• Asking follow-up questions that demonstrate interest and the desire for clarity
• Letting people speak until they feel they are finished
• Summarising to show that you have been listening and want to demonstrate that what was said matters to you.
• Following up the same topic rather than immediately switching to a different topic of interest only to you.

Remember as always the fundamental values, vision, aims and rationale that are driving you and your colleagues in the first place. If you do that, then you will be determined to find the best way of communicating, deciding and chairing meetings,

Techniques and tools for involving colleagues

The audit stage of planning *(see Session 5)* provides a great opportunity for you to work with colleagues to clarify your philosophy and aims and to assess how well you are doing. Techniques such as *Thought showering, Nominal Group Technique* and *SWOT* analysis may also engage the interest of colleagues.

Thought Showering

Team members contribute ideas about how to deal with any given issue by suggesting all and any ideas that come to mind about the topic in question for a couple of minutes. Ideas are rapidly listed without comment and value judgements are deferred. Typically folk run out of ideas after a minute or two. Then it is time to use the list that has been created as a basis for discussions about the quality of the ideas and as a basis for coming to decisions about what is to be done.

Nominal Group Technique

Nominal group technique is a variation of the thought showering technique. The leader invites all group members to spend a couple of minutes writing down all their suggestions about a given issue on post-its, one idea per post-it. Thereafter members of the group stick one post-it at a time in rotation onto a board or flipchart. As before, no evaluative comment should be made until all ideas have been posted in their turn The next step is for the leader to review the list of ideas, post-it by post-it, inviting discussion of each suggestion by asking questions, statements of clarification, or statements of agreement or disagreement regarding the relevance of the ideas to the issue in question. After this discussion, the relevance or value of ideas can be short-listed through a preliminary vote before final choices are made.

SWOT Analysis

SWOT Analysis is a strategic planning tool used to evaluate the Strengths, Weaknesses, Opportunities, and Threats involved in a project. Specifically:

- Strengths are *internal* attributes of the school that are helpful to achieving the objective.

- Weaknesses are *internal* attributes of the school that are harmful to achieving the objective.

- Opportunities are *external* conditions that help achieve the objective.

- Threats are *external* conditions that are harmful to achieving the objective.

Normally these are listed in a simple diagram under the appropriate headings. Then it is a matter of deciding how to exploit each strength and opportunity and how to minimise each weakness and threat.

Workshop Session 4(a): Communication and decision-making

Workshop Session 4(a): Communication:

Introduction

As *Thought Piece 4(a):1* on communication makes clear, poor communication lies at the heart of many damaged relationships between team leaders and their colleagues, with a consequential reduction ultimately in the effectiveness of learning and teaching. Colleagues have their own responsibility to ensure that they are both reading and hearing correctly and expressing themselves clearly but, as always, there is a special onus on the team leader to create the kind of climate of trust in which people are valued and encouraged to express their own views.

Trust

When people feel trusted, they are much more likely to seek clarification of something they are not sure of or to engage in the kind of open debate that can lead to agreed meaning. They will trust their leader if there is consistency between what the leader preaches and what the leader practises – even when they do not necessarily agree with what the leader preaches. Leaders who say one thing and do another will find that their messages are not taken at face value. In this connection, the links between effective communication and effective motivation seem obvious.

Decision-making: Introduction

A key skill in becoming a successful leader is the skill of decision making. It is surprising how many leaders do not like taking decisions. They do all kinds of things to keep the moment of decision at arms length including: gathering more data, talking to more people, not thinking about the decision, fretting over who the decision might offend, worrying about the resources needed to implement the decision and so on. Good leaders develop the skill of making the best decision possible with the best information possible in the timeliest manner.

Learning Outcomes

By the end of this section of the session readers will have:

- ✓ Read over a number of thought pieces related to communication and decision-making

- ✓ Reviewed the key skills required in identifying and reducing barriers to communication

- ✓ Reviewed the nature of the decision-making, decision-taking process

Workshop Session 4 (a): Communication and decision-making

Thought Piece 4(a) 1: The Importance of Effective Communication

It is impossible to exaggerate how important it is for a team leader to be able to communicate effectively. Look at any of the professional actions expected of effective team leaders, or for that matter at any of the three key elements that underpin practice and it is obvious that the ability to communicate effectively underpins all of them.

Communication is, of course, not just about sending out messages but about receiving messages. It is of critical importance to realise that what the sender says is not nearly as important as what the receiver hears. Senders and receivers both have a duty to make sure that a message is understood but team leaders have a particular responsibility for trying to make sure that meaning is communicated effectively. A failure to communicate properly often leads to a breakdown in relationships – and such a breakdown can make it all the more difficult to communicate effectively next time around.

Reducing Barriers to Effective Communication: Values, ethics and skills

Earlier thought pieces discussed the link between motivation and the quality of interpersonal relationships. Effective communication also depends above all upon the quality of such relationships. Team leaders can often remove barriers, prevent breakdowns of communication and improve communication effectiveness by:

1) Establishing effective interpersonal relationships
2) Managing position power
3) Acquiring feedback
4) Being active listeners
5) Displaying empathy
6) Understanding the ethics of conversation

Interpersonal Relationships

We have already discussed the importance of leadership style in establishing good interpersonal relationships. If the members of a team have a poor relationship with the team leader, or with each other, then there is likely to be reduced respect for each other's judgement. In such cases the quality and quantity of information that people are willing to share with each other is likely to be reduced. As a result, it may be that issues simply do not get an adequate airing, leading to a reduced quality of decision-making (See the next topic)

For all of these reasons it is essential for the team leader to build a climate of trust. Such a climate is created when the leader is consistent in words, actions and deeds. Where there is such consistency, colleagues are much more likely to accept the sincerity of the leader's communications. In such a climate too the members of the team are more likely to trust each other. Accordingly they communicate more directly, more openly and more fully.

Position power

Like interpersonal relations, power and its use, or perhaps more properly its abuse, can have a serious effect on the quality of communication. Leaders are in a position to reward or punish individuals and those who inspire fear rather than respect should not be surprised if colleagues decline to communicate fully to them their ideas, their hopes or their fears.

A surprisingly common problem is when a leader sincerely believes that he or she is a democratic and participatory leader, always ready to consult colleagues and take their ideas on board when in fact he or she is perceived as an autocrat by other colleagues. It is a thoughtful leader who checks out the way he or she is perceived rather than possibly deluding himself or herself. Certainly colleagues will avoid responding honestly to a leader if they think an invitation to express their views is likely to lead to a sharp reaction if those views do not happen to coincide with the views of the leader.

Acquiring Feedback

Team leaders should regularly seek feedback from colleagues. It is important to remember that many teachers have excellent ideas about how to improve programmes of study and methods of teaching, and effective leaders establish channels for that information to reach them. Once the channels are in place they use them to define roles, motivate and empower individuals and manage conflict. They seek the opinions and concerns of colleagues and provide them with a comfort level that will help them to express their true feelings about the messages that are being communicated.

Practising Active Listening

Active listening means acquiring the total meaning of a message and observing the underlying feelings, while noting and being sensitive to all verbal and non-verbal clues displayed by the sender. A team leader who continues to file folders in a filing cabinet, while assuring a colleague that he or she is listening to the concerns that the colleague wants to explore with the leader, is seriously insulting that colleague. The active listener concentrates on the speaker, uses probing questions to clarify the sender's concerns and by appropriate eye contact, nods and gestures shows empathy for the colleague in question. Not only will the sender appreciate such active listening but he or she will be more likely to display similar active listening to other colleagues.

Displaying Empathy

Followers tend to be receptive to leaders who display empathy in the communication process. Empathy means being able to put oneself in the position of another person. An important aspect of empathy involves the receiver conveying to the sender that their feelings are acknowledged and understood and that both the meaning and the feeling behind what is being said are appreciated. By using empathy, a leader can demonstrate a spirit of genuine respect for the worth of the individual. The possibilities of arriving at a team approach to resolving problems are enhanced accordingly.

The Ethics of Conversation

When individuals participate in ethical conversations, the conversation is governed by reason. Participants are willing to provide evidence to back up their views, take responsibility for what they say, be open to persuasion and yield to the better argument. Effective dialogue presumes that all participants are equally open to persuasion and will yield to the better argument. If agreement cannot be reached, agreeing to disagree, while respecting the other viewpoint, is an important aid to progress. Related to the issue of ethics is the matter of discretion. Much damage has been done to interpersonal relationships by indiscrete and ill-judged remarks. For a leader to be indiscrete is a particularly serious flaw.

Reducing Barriers to Effective Communication: Technical Issues

The section above focuses very much on the necessary values or ethics of the leader and on the kind of interpersonal skills that have already been noted in the Standard for Team Leadership. Not least of these is the ability to adapt the method and style of communication to the situation. There are again echoes of the issues of leadership style here.

Other common barriers to effective communication, apart from the overall quality of interpersonal relationships, include the following:

Information overload: Familiar enough! People receive so much information that they simply cannot take it all in. This can be especially common with regard to written communications (even when it is emailed) People may fail to read everything that has come their way and may miss vital information. To add insult to injury they may complain of lack of consultation and blame the leader for not alerting them - even when it is pointed out to them that the memo or paper in question was placed in their pigeon-holes or emailed to them on such and such a date.

Differences in status: Conveying and conferring meaning on a communication may be inhibited simply because the sender and the receiver occupy different positions in the school's hierarchy. A junior colleague may hesitate to seek clarification from a senior colleague because they fear looking stupid in the eyes of the senior person, not least when that person will be writing review or promotion reports upon them. The very existence of a hierarchy will tend to emphasise differences of interpretation, not least between leaders and teacher representatives. The greater the disparity in status, the more likely is it that effective communication will not take place.

Semantics: Different words have different meanings for different people. Words may also have no meaning for some people. And the English language is in itself a rich source of ambiguity. Professional colleagues can confuse each other – and parents might not have a clue about the jargon used by teachers who in their turn either do not seem to realise the technical nature of the language they are using - or are using it deliberately in an attempt to impress.

Filtering: This refers to a situation in which the message from the original sender is altered, intentionally or otherwise, by an intermediary or only partially communicated to the receiver. Filtering can cause quite serious problems in those cases where a message is passed down through a hierarchical structure and individuals at each level confer their own meaning on what they heard or read before passing it on to the next receiver. There can also be unfortunate delays as messages are passed down through the system with receivers picking them up too late to act upon them.

Body language or paralanguage: Meaning may be conveyed – and indeed conferred- by such simple signs as a raised eyebrow, a long look, a momentary silence and by such vocal signs as speed of speech and a variety of grunts and sighs. There is plenty of scope for confusion if such indicators are at odds with the actual words being spoken. Indeed research would seem to indicate that receivers confer much more meaning on the basis of *how* things are said than on *what* is said. The sender might be very well aware of this in the first place of course and manipulate the message accordingly.

Time: It is often forgotten that communication can take up lots of time. It might be desirable for a team leader to try and make sure that everything is conveyed to colleagues in a personal one-to-one way as a means of promoting not only clarity of meaning but good interpersonal relationships. This may be relatively easy when the team is small. But, to take one example, a pastoral leader in a large secondary school who wants to make sure that all of Margaret's teachers are made personally aware of how distressed she is about a family matter and about possible behavioural consequences might need a whole morning to achieve her purposes.

In addition to the interpersonal strategies already noted that may be used to prevent or reduce barriers to communication, there is a simple list of rules to keep in mind if we wish to overcome the more technical barriers to communication that have been mentioned (although it is worth noting that while it may be easy to enunciate a few simple rules, their proper application in different contexts is a much more complex matter) Thus we should:

- Have a clear understanding of what we want to say and then say it in simple, clear, unambiguous ways
- Use a style that is acceptable and understandable to the receiver
- Explain why we may be issuing certain requests for action and the precise steps that we would like to be taken
- Avoid telling people too much at once
- Categorise the importance of given communications
- Match the time taken to the importance of the communication

- Clarify the relationship between the aims of the communication and the hoped for outcomes
- Be consistent in what we say and do

The rapidly extending use of ICT within and between schools and the individual teachers within them offers remarkable opportunities for improving the visibility and transparency of information that is shared between leaders and managers. ICT may also increase the possibility of communication responsiveness and collaborative working by integrating available knowledge and reducing the possibility of misunderstandings, deliberate or otherwise. At the same time there is the risk that the sheer convenience of a tool like email might increase the possibility of information overload. And it goes almost without saying that there is not a lot of difference between the teacher who fails to check email and the one who fails to check a pigeon-hole.

Team-based communications

Schools are social systems and as such people within them have various means of exchanging information. Thought Piece 2.5 deals with leading and building teams and here we look at three different communication networks that may be used to connect senders and receivers within a team setting – the 'chain', the 'radial' and the 'circle' networks.

In the 'chain', the flow of the communication is essentially top-down, with messages being sent down the 'chain of command'. In the 'radial', a team leader discusses issues singly with each team member in turn. In the 'circle' all members of the team are able to discuss issues with each other at a team meeting.

The chain network is obviously associated with hierarchical structures and a line management approach. Simple communications or straightforward tasks can be communicated in this way but even at that there may be low morale at the bottom end of the chain as people feel that they are forever being told what to do and never being asked what they would like to do.

The radial network may well be used by a team leader who is interested in getting individual views from different team members about a given issue. It is helpful for speaking – and listening - to quiet colleagues who do not speak up at meetings or who may tend to conform in public situations to the majority view on any topic.

The circle network seems most effective for dealing with complex issues and clearly offers the possibility of the team leader using team meetings (See again Session 3 on meetings) to build a collaborative culture in which the views of all colleagues are sought, shared and valued. It is important, however to make sure that it is not always the one voice that dominates team meetings. So sometimes it might be a good idea to use the radial instead – or at least as well.

Thought Piece 4(a) 2: Decision-making: Decision-taking

Decision-making may be defined as a systematic process of choosing from several alternatives to achieve a desired result. Decision – taking is concerned with who it is who actually takes the decision at the end of the decision-making process. There are three elements within this definition of decision –making: (a) Choosing among options (b) the nature of the decision-making process and (c) the purpose or desired outcome of the decision.

Choosing among options has far reaching implications. A decision typically involves acceptance of one proposal and rejection of another. If, for example, a decision means that one teacher is provided with a resource or opportunity at the expense of another teacher, then the potential for negative reaction, at least on the part of the unsuccessful teacher, are obvious. It is therefore essential for a leader to make informed choices, to act with integrity and to be ready to explain why certain decisions were taken – or not taken.

So far as the decision-making process is concerned, a leader may take decisions independently or by involving others. There will be times when the leader has sufficient knowledge to make the decision independently but more often than not the quality of a decision and its acceptance will be enhanced by the involvement of others.

With regard to the involvement of others, decision-making is based on the fundamental principle that individuals who should be involved in the process should include:

- Those who are affected by the decision

- Those who have the knowledge and expertise to contribute to the process

- Those who are responsible for implementing the decision

In general, the purpose of an inclusive decision-making process is to meet the needs of pupils while empowering school staffs by inviting them to contribute to any decision that they will be called upon to implement. Such empowerment is likely to enhance their commitment to making the decision work.

Key Elements

School-based decision-making rests on two well-established propositions:

1. The school is the primary decision-making unit; and decisions should be made at the lowest possible level.

2. Change requires ownership that comes from the opportunity to participate in defining change and the flexibility to adapt it to individual circumstances. As Michael Fullan so consistently argues, change cannot be mandated from outside.

These propositions are based upon the assumption that those who best understand the needs of pupils, their learning styles and their levels of performance are better positioned to make decisions about educational matters than those farther removed from the teaching and learning process. For school-based decision-making to work there are three key requirements:

1. Those to be involved need appropriate knowledge and skills. Pooled ignorance does not contribute to effective decision-making.

2. A collegiate approach is required whereby individuals are willing and to work in a team approach to resolve differences of view and flexible enough to accept final decisions even if they do not reflect their own preferences.

3. Those to be involved in the decision-making process and in particular those who actually take the final decision, must have the necessary power and authority to do so.

Decision-Making Structures

Schools embracing shared decision-making typically develop various forums in which proposed major decisions can be debated. These include whole staff, senior management team and departmental meetings, cross-curricular meetings and meetings that involve other stakeholders such as parents, pupils and support staff. Subcommittees that include representation from a range of stakeholders are often set up and these allow for an extended range of perceptions. Schools that engage in shared decision-making also set aside time for teachers to meet and places for them to congregate and talk. In addition, school timetables are often designed to facilitate teacher interaction by structuring common planning periods.

Selecting a Decision Making Style

Typically there are four decision making styles again related to the kinds of leadership styles discussed earlier in *Thought Piece 2.4(b)*

1. **Autocratic**: The leader reaches a decision without any assistance from followers. Followers therefore have no influence over decisions.

2. **Consultative**: The leader seeks the opinion of followers and asks them for their ideas. After giving consideration to the ideas, opinions, and suggestions of subordinates, the leader makes the decision.

3. **Joint Decision Making**: The leader meets with followers, discusses the problem, and together they develop a workable solution to the problem. The leader serves as a group participant and has no more influence than any other member of the group.

4. **Distributive**: The leader gives authority and responsibility for making the decision to the group. Limits are specified, and prior approval may or may not be required for decision implementation.

Three other aspects are worthy of consideration in the decision-making process:

a) **Quality and acceptance**
b) **Degree of concern**
c) **Level of decision**

(a) Quality and acceptance
The *quality* of a decision depends upon the contribution that participants bring to the decision making process. As was noted earlier, it is doubtful for example if there is much point in involving

people in the making of a decision if they simply do not have the necessary knowledge and expertise. Nevertheless it is always wise to allow individuals to make that call for themselves rather than deciding on their behalf that they do not possess the necessary knowledge or skill to contribute to a given decision-making situation.

Acceptance refers to the degree to which followers are committed to implementing a decision in an effective manner. In some instances, decisions will be accepted by followers simply because it is beneficial to them or because of the approach used by the leader in reaching the decision. In other cases, followers may refuse to accept a decision, even if it makes sense, because it was made in an autocratic manner.

(b) Degree of concern

A decision is relevant to the concerns of followers to the extent to which they are affected by it or expected to be involved in the implementation process. It seems obvious that leaders should always involve colleagues in any decision-making process that they will be called upon to implement. Conversely if decisions are outside the interest of followers then they are not likely to be highly motivated to participate in the decision making process. Accordingly their exclusion from that process is unlikely to affect either the quality or acceptance of the decision in question. That said, it is a wise idea to leave it to individuals to decide how much a decision matters to them rather than deciding for them.

(c) Level of decision

It is useful to distinguish among three levels of decision-making: strategic, tactical and operational.

Strategic decisions are concerned with the long–term philosophy, direction or vision of a school. Such decisions are usually taken by the head teacher or by a senior colleague on behalf of the head teacher although it may well be that the decision has been taken at local authority or government level in which case the head teacher is called upon to support the implementation of that decision at individual school level. Arguably, too, middle and senior managers can take long-term strategic decisions about, say, curricular structure or the delivery of programmes of study within the curricular structure, so long as the decisions are within the parameters of overall philosophy and strategy.

124

Another useful way of thinking of strategic decisions is in terms of the number of different people who are likely to be affected over time by the consequences of such decisions. The greater the number of people likely to be affected, the more strategic is the nature of the decision and the higher the authority required to sanction the decision.

Tactical decisions focus more on medium-term issues and may be made by senior or middle managers. Typically such decisions relate to the priorities that a school or department has for the achievement of its strategic goals. School improvement planning involves many tactical decisions with senior staff deciding on what the priorities are for the next year or two so far as the whole school is concerned and with heads of department coming to similar decisions so far as their own department is concerned. A senior school leader deciding that it is time to focus on whole school methods of assessment or a departmental head deciding to adopt a new text or teaching method is making a tactical decision.

Operational decisions focus on day-to-day activities within the school and are typically made by all levels of teacher, including those who are not promoted. Decisions made at this level help to ensure that daily activities proceed smoothly and therefore help to move the school toward reaching its strategic goals. Examples of operational decisions include the decisions that a teacher makes on the choice of topics to deal with on a given day and the materials, lesson planning and delivery that is considered to be appropriate.

One very important issue relating to decision- taking levels is the matter of appropriateness. It is inappropriate, time-consuming and ultimately unprofessional for senior school leaders to be forever taking decisions for classroom teachers that they are perfectly capable of taking for themselves. All teachers have a range of accountabilities that relate to their levels of seniority and part of being accountable is the right to take decisions in the first place. And accountability cannot be delegated. A senior leader who blunders over some decision cannot blame junior colleagues even if it was they who suggested the decision in the first place. By the same token, it is vital for all teachers not to take decisions that are 'ultra vires' – beyond their powers. Much damage can be caused by teachers arbitrarily deciding to take some action that runs counter to agreed procedures, especially if those procedures have been agreed at a higher level.

This concludes the thought pieces for Session 4.

Session 4(a): Workshop Activities

Activity WS4(a)1: Communication scenarios

Look again at *Thought Piece 4(a) 1*, in particular the section dealing with the various kinds of barriers to effective communication. Answer these questions with regard to the scenarios that follow.

    i.   What types of barrier were there, in terms of relationships and/or technical issues, to effective communication in each case?

    ii.   How might they have been avoided in the first place?

    iii.   What should the leader need to do now in an effort to retrieve the situation?

The first set of scenarios is relevant to aspiring middle managers.

The second set of scenarios is relevant to aspiring senior managers

Share your views with colleagues if possible.

Set 1 (aspiring middle managers)

Scenario 1(a)

A teacher overheard her head of department criticising her teaching ability to a senior management colleague. The head of department had never said anything to her about the quality of her work.

Scenario 2(a)

A new team leader took up her appointment in a new school and was surprised to note that team meetings were very infrequent and tended to deal with simple matters of administration that could just be as easily covered by an email and attachment. For her, teamwork and meetings went pretty well hand in hand, with meetings being seen as a great opportunity to build team spirit and a common commitment. Her retiring predecessor tipped her off that there was a war-weary cynic in the department who would use any and all meetings as a platform for his views, much to the (silent) irritation of other members of the department who were more committed. So eventually her predecessor had decided to stop having meetings.

Scenario 3(a)

A team leader called a quick team meeting to issue details about various administrative requirements, including the return date for pupil assessments so that deadlines for sending reports out to parents could be met. In the event one teacher did not submit assessments at the next meeting as required. The team leader did not hold a high opinion of the teacher's competence at the best of times and somewhat abruptly demanded an explanation at the next meeting for the non return of assessments. The teacher pointed out that she had been called away the previous time because of a family bereavement and had not received a copy of the necessary return dates. It had not occurred to her to ask anyone about what had happened at the previous meeting, partially because she had other things on her mind and also for the simple reason that she did not know that a meeting had been held. She was angry at the unwarranted public criticism.

Scenario 4(a)

A teacher checked her pigeon –hole and found a memo from the school time-tabler to the effect that she would be receiving an additional teaching period in two weeks time. The reasons for allocating the extra teaching period were given in the memo and there was no question of non-contact time agreements being breached. The teacher was seen to read the memo before storming out of the staffroom, slamming the door behind her.

Scenario 5(a)

A head teacher announced at a whole school meeting that she would be launching a period of consultation with staff, parents and pupils on the possibility of revising the structure of the curriculum and the school day in line with the principles enunciated in *A Curriculum for Excellence*. The gossip in the staffroom, led by one or two cynics, was that the decision had already been taken and that the consultation process would be a sham and not worth participating in. One of the cynics is a member of the department that you lead.

Set 2 (aspiring senior managers)

Scenario 1(b)

A teacher was very upset when she overheard her departmental head criticising her teaching ability to the link SMT member. She was even more upset when the SMT link agreed and even added words of further criticism. Neither had ever said anything to her about the quality of her work.

Scenario 2(b)

At an SMT meeting, members drew up a final draft of next session's whole school calendar of planned meetings for consultation with staff. A keen new depute head, allocated the guidance remit, used the draft next day to draw up detailed proposals for the timing of guidance meetings and issued them at a guidance team meeting. A member of the guidance team mentioned the meeting to colleagues in the staff room. The HT quickly gathered from the 'grapevine' that teachers were unhappy about apparently not being consulted about next session's calendar of events.

Scenario 3(b)

The DHT with responsibility in the school for the timetable and absence cover was given the name of an art teacher who was very interested in an impending vacancy in the school for two days of cover per week for several months. The DHT contacted the teacher but the days on offer coincided with other commitments that the teacher had. The DHT assured the teacher that the art department timetable could be revised to suit the teacher's availability and he would get back to the teacher at a later date. Some time later, the supply teacher phoned the HT to find out what was happening. Knowing nothing, the HT sought clarification from the DHT. It transpired that the DHT had not been able to adjust the timetable to fit the teacher's availability as promised but had not told anyone.

Scenario 4(b)

One Wednesday, an SMT were discussing plans for an induction day the following Monday for primary 7 pupils. It was agreed that lists of the new S1 class groupings would be issued to parents ahead of the event. Upon reflection, the depute head who was organising the induction day privately decided to issue class lists to the pupils on the morning of the induction day, having remembered that, the previous year, there had been several phone calls from parents demanding that their children be allocated to different classes from the ones proposed. The first anyone knew of the change was when the first part of the induction programme had to be given over to the extended reading out of new class lists.

Scenario 5(b)

After extensive discussion among themselves about the pros and cons of mixed ability and setting, an SMT decide to introduce setting across the subject board in order to promote more direct teaching, despite the preference of one DHT to retain mixed ability groupings so that pupils would not be labelled. At a meeting with heads of department to announce the decision, the HT was taken aback when several heads of department objected to the proposal and quoted the views of the SMT member in support of their concerns.

Activity WS4(a)2: Decision-making scenario (aspiring middle managers)

A few years ago, as part of a leadership development programme on decision-making, a group of aspiring managers were invited to think of an occasion when they took a strategic decision that went well or badly. They were invited to describe the basic situation and the choices that were open to them, the decision-making style that they adopted and why, the decision that they took and the consequences of their decision. Two aspiring mangers provided the decision-making scenarios that are described below. Read their reports and then analyse how they handled things by answering the questions that follow the second scenario. You might find it useful to read *Thought Piece 4(a) 2* again

Decision-making scenario (aspiring to middle management)

Basic situation: I was appointed as the new head of a modern languages department of five teachers, having served for eight years as a respected and very successful classroom teacher in another school. A number of aspects of the new department concerned me – not least the dated materials and dated rote-learning methods that were being used in the department and the lack of effective use of ICT as a modern teaching tool. The overall approach seemed to me to be somewhat elitist, with little in the way of appropriate approaches for less able pupils. I was aware that the department had received a negative HMI report recently for these reasons.

Choices available: I could leave the status quo - and ironically enough examination performance in modern languages was above national levels of performance - I could begin by updating materials and methods in SI with a view to rolling out further changes in later years or I could go for a root and branch change to materials and methods throughout the department.

Decision-making style: I expressed my concerns to my new departmental colleagues at my first departmental meeting with them and invited them to share their views with me. There was considerable resentment among staff about the HMI report and a lot of defensiveness. They saw themselves as a conscientious group of teachers whose pupils had gained respectable results over the years and they saw no great need for change, other than perhaps not allowing less able pupils to study a modern language.

Quality of decision: I decided that there was not much point in debating the issues as attitudes seemed to be inflexible. So I decided that there should be a radical change in materials and methods starting the following session and approached the head teacher for additional funding. With this granted, I ordered extensive new materials for every year group and proposed to set aside a number of departmental meetings to explain to staff how to use these new materials. I felt this was a good decision as I could not accept that pupils should be short-changed any longer.

Acceptance of decision: Nothing was said to my face but I could see my colleagues were not happy. But I thought they would come round in time as I was sure the new materials and methods were a significant improvement on the old ones and pupils - and staff - would love them.

Level of decision

I saw this as a strategic decision that I had the right to take as a departmental leader.

Decision-making scenario (aspiring to senior management)

Basic situation: For several years the school had organised six parents' reporting nights per annum in line with local and national agreements. Parental attendance was not high although all staff turned out for all nights as required. As acting HT (the HT was on secondment) I was approached by the three teacher representatives in the school and they suggested that we should reduce the parents' reporting nights to 3 in number, one for S1/S2, one for S3/S4 and one for S5/S6 instead of one for each of the six year groups

Choices available: I could leave the status quo, I could agree to the proposal of the teacher reps or I could go for some compromise situation.

Decision-making style: I invited the reps to an SMT meeting to state their case and to listen to counter arguments before coming to a decision. I also checked with the school janitor about adequacy of accommodation if we were potentially to double numbers of parents attending by cutting the number of nights. I also discussed the possibilities with my SMT.

Quality of decision: I decided to reduce the number of parents' reporting nights from 6 to 4, one for S1, one for S2 options, one for S3/S4 and one for S5/S6. Everyone had agreed that a reduction in parents' nights was desirable and manageable so that staff could spend more time on general lesson preparation and correction rather than sitting around waiting for parents who did not turn up.

Acceptance of decision: Staff were happy enough with the compromise solution and I was pleased with my decision-making skills.

Level of decision: I saw this as a strategic decision. Although I was only the acting HT, the HT was on a two-year secondment and it seemed to me appropriate that I should come to a firm decision on this matter as planning for the session ahead was about to begin.

Decision-making scenario; Analysis
Using each of the headings in these reports (basic situation etc) describe your own reactions to the ways in which the aspiring leaders went about the business of coming to a decision in each case. Do you agree that these were indeed strategic decisions? If so, are you satisfied that all of the implications were duly considered? What would you have done and why?

Feedback: Activity WS4 (a)1: Communication Scenarios

The 'solutions' to each of the various scenarios may very well vary depending on the kind of leaders involved and the context and it is useful to consider how issues might be dealt with in different ways. But most of the issues involved the leader in apologising for insensitivity and thoughtlessness. Among the most frequently occurring comments about the individual scenarios from previous readers or course participants are the following:

Set 1(aspiring middle managers):

Scenario 1(a):

Most people comment on the apparently unethical nature of the decision of the head of department to discuss matters with a senior colleague and not directly with the teacher in question. It looks very much as if the head of department is avoiding responsibilities and indulging in destructive gossip. Commentators are much less critical when it transpires that the head of department was simply seeking advice from the senior colleague about how best to handle the situation – and assured the teacher of this before going on to discuss with the teacher possible CPD solutions. See also a similar scenario in the set for aspiring senior managers.

Scenario 2(a):

Most people agree that it is time to re-introduce meetings and for the new head of department to brush up appropriate chairing skills. In particular most agree that the departmental head should seek an early opportunity to have a conversation with the cynic – inviting the cynic to explain his or her attitudes and then seeking to secure his or her commitment to departmental aims and objectives, not least by making clear to the cynic the potential benefits of his or her extended experience and abilities.

Scenario 3(a):

Most people consider that the head of department is well out of order here. The teacher in question could well take out a formal grievance against the head of department. If there are pre-existing concerns about the competence of the teacher, what if anything has the head of department done to improve things? The department head is so ill-disposed towards this colleague that he/she has failed to realise that it was entirely his or her fault that the teacher knew nothing about deadlines, having missed the hastily-convened meeting. Even if warranted, the criticism should have been in private, with support offered. At the very least, a public apology to the teacher is essential.

Scenario 4(a):

Most people consider that the school timetable expert was within his or her rights to make the time table change in question. But the strong view is that such a change should have been explained to the teacher face-to-face. Either the timetabler is avoiding a confrontation in a way that can only make worse or is so insensitive as not to realise that he/she owes the teacher at least the courtesy of a personal explanation. There is also the view that the timetabler should have explained matters directly both to the teacher and to the head of department, for whom the changed timetable of the teacher is likely to have some consequences.

Scenario 5(a):

As with Scenario 2, the common view is that the head of department should tackle the cynic head on. He or she should be invited to justify the remarks made. At the same time, the head of department should make it clear that he/she intends to involve the department fully in the consultation process. If in due course there is some reason to feel that the cynic has a point then the head of department should make it clear that he or she will be happy to raise legitimate concerns with the HT on behalf of the department.

Set 2 (aspiring senior managers)

Scenario 1(b)

This was actually a different occasion to scenario 1 in set 1. Both team leaders are badly at fault. The SMT member should of course be advising the departmental head to raise concerns directly with the teacher and offering support rather than indulging in such behaviour. The teacher in this case raised a grievance and both team leaders received written warnings as to their future conduct. Relationships were never really restored until the teacher retired several years later.

Scenario 2(b):

The new DIIT is rather rash here in his/her enthusiasm to get on with organising meetings. The unfortunate fact here was that there was anyway a tendency on the part of staff to complain about not being consulted that the HT, also new, was trying to overcome. Assurances were given to the staff about consultation in future and the HT had a few words of wisdom for the DHT.

Scenario 3(b):
There is of course here a complete failure to communicate at all. It would have been sensible for the DHT to let the HT know about the possibilities, not least given the importance of trying to fill a key staffing vacancy. In the event, no other supply art teacher was found and the education of pupils suffered accordingly.

Scenario 4(b)

Here is another bad example of non-communication. Whatever the concerns of the DHT about belated memories of events a year earlier, he/she not have gone ahead and changed the agreed arrangements without full discussion. What the DHT did led to a great deal of quite unnecessary resentment on the induction day.

Scenario 5(b)

The SMT is rather like the Cabinet in that collective responsibility should be observed. Whatever one's individual views, they should be subordinated to the final team decision. If the decision to introduce setting across the subject board is not the correct one then this should become evident in time and the SMT member in favour of mixed ability class arrangements will have another opportunity to put across his or her points. That said, a number of previous readers and course members have pointed out that the HT should have included subject leaders in the consultation in the first place and not confined it only to SMT members.

Feedback: Activity WS4(a)2: Decision-making scenarios

The most common comments about the two scenarios that were submitted by previous readers and programme participants are provided below. There is a also a brief note on what happened next in each case.

Decision-making scenario; aspiring middle managers: Analysis

Basic situation:

The basic situation seems clear enough. Obviously the new head of department would rightly be keen to review current programmes and methods and seems to have been justified about the concerns described. However the new departmental head should have spent much more time chatting to new colleagues about the situation and finding out more about what colleagues thought of things, what pupils thought of things and what parents thought of things.

Choices available:
Leaving the status quo does not seem to be a viable option, not least given the concerns expressed by HMI and their proposal to return in due course to review developments. A root and branch review of all programmes is likely to be too much for staff to undertake. A pilot programme with say S1, with the promise of further review

before rolling out the programme across the school might be the most sensible option.

Decision-making style:

There seems to have been a limited amount of consultation and the general impression is that the new head of department was determined to press ahead with a radical programme no matter what. There seems to have little serious effort to win hearts and minds by considering staff views and by thinking through the implications of taking on such a large change if there was staff opposition.

Quality of decision:

No doubt the departmental head was right to institute changes but the proposed pace of change seems to be a case of too much too soon

Acceptance of decision:

It seems clear that staff were not happy and that would make the successful introduction of the necessary changes much more fraught with the possibility of failure

Level of decision:

This decision can reasonably be described as a strategic decision. The implications for all departmental staff and all pupils are very considerable for the years ahead. The head of department may well be operating within his or her levels of authority but would be better advised to bring staff along in seeking to implement such a major set of changes by phasing in more slowly new materials and methods with which staff are not familiar.

Decision-making scenario; aspiring senior managers: Analysis

Basic situation:

The first step should have been to check out local and national agreements. The HT would need to be careful about not acting beyond his powers by coming to a decision about parents' nights that breached such agreements – especially if that meant reducing the number of such nights that parents locally had become used to. As a matter of courtesy also the acting HT should have contacted the seconded HT and sought his advice before proceeding possibly to alter an agreement that he had originally negotiated – no doubt with good reason.

Choices available:

If there was genuine concern about the value of having quite so many reporting nights, it might have been an idea to drop one night by combining the S5/S6 reporting night and then introducing a prize-giving night or possibly an open night for parents to view displays of pupils' work, thus still retaining the original number of parents' nights but varying their purpose.

Decision-making style:
Most folk would certainly have consulted staff as the acting HT did, and checking out practical matters like the logistics of joint parents' nights made sense. But most folk would also have consulted the parents' and pupils' councils. The acting HT seems to have forgotten that not all stakeholders are members of staff. As noted, it would have been an idea to double-check with the seconded head before proceeding at all and probably also to check with local divisional offices to clarify the parameters within which the acting HT could proceed.

Quality of decision:

Initially, the decision to compromise seems quite a sensible one. Staff would probably work hard to ensure that the new format of parents' nights would be every bit as useful to parents as the old format. And no doubt they would be happy to be busier on the nights in question. But what about the views of parents? What was their reaction when they were informed that in future there would only be four parents' nights per annum and not six?

Acceptance of decision:

Staff seemed reasonably happy, understandably enough - but again what about acceptance by parents? Would they accept a decision about such an important matter without being consulted?

Level of decision:

An acting HT, especially one who is likely to be in post during a two-year secondment of the serving head, is rightly the final decision-maker here, within the limits of the powers of any head.

Post script to the scenarios
In the first scenario, the modern languages staff complained to their trade union representative about excessive workload demands from all the changes proposed by the new departmental head and

the representative complained to the HT, pointing that at least one member of department was considering taking out an official grievance as he had been very successful with pupil performance over many years and deeply resented the criticism of his efforts, as he saw it, that was implied within all these proposed changes. The HT suggested that the head of department should phase in changes gradually and work harder to win hearts and minds.

In the second scenario, the day after the decision about the revised number of parents' nights was announced, a parent contacted the acting HT to complain about lack of consultation and the fact that, as a caring parent, she would not now have the same amount of time to discuss her S4 daughter's progress towards national exams as she had previously. She intended to complain to divisional offices. The acting HT contacted the offices personally and was advised to suspend the decision pending a full and proper discussion with all interested parties. And whatever the final decision was, it would be important not to undermine local and national agreements about parents' nights.

Session 4 (b) Managing Conflict

Session 4 (b): Managing Conflict

Introduction

So far we have been consistently focusing upon the scope that we have as leaders for motivating our colleagues and team-building and the powerful benefits that a collaborative and collegial approach can bring for all concerned. Yet as staff, parents and pupils increasingly insist on their rights, contractual or otherwise, and are increasingly willing to challenge other viewpoints then the potential for conflict and even litigation rises significantly.

Dealing with what often seem to be intractable interpersonal problems is probably the most challenging task facing any leader. In this part of the session we shall look at managing difficult people as a means of looking at managing conflict generally.

The Nature of Conflict

It should be noted immediately that conflict that involves honest differences of opinion over alternative courses of action is positive and helpful. Such 'functional' conflict relates to the 'storming' stage of the team-building process and to the decision-making process that we have been discussing and can help the quality and acceptability of final decisions by ensuring that all the possibilities are fully considered.

'Dysfunctional' conflict is something different and tends to arise when the debate focuses on individuals and their emotions and when one or more of the individuals involved adopt inflexible positions on key issues. There is a fear of losing 'face', a win-lose attitude develops, hostility increases as the conflict becomes more bitter, team spirit is badly damaged and before long the education of the pupils is at risk.

Clearly, team leaders need to be able to understand the nature and context of conflict and to develop the skills that will help to remove, or at least reduce, its harmful effects.

Learning Outcomes

By the end of this section of the session you will have:

✓ Read over a number of thought pieces about the nature of conflict

✓ Reflected on the management of conflict and difficult people

✓ Identified the key leadership skills, the principles and the steps that are required to remove or at least reduce such conflicts.

N.B. In this workshop the activities for aspiring middle managers and aspiring senior managers are differentiated but unsurprisingly the skills, principles and general steps that either should consider in dealing with conflict and difficult people are essentially the same. Indeed aspiring middle managers and senior managers might look over both activities.

Thought Piece 4(b): Managing Conflict:

Sources of conflict

Interpersonal conflicts are actually quite common and are liable to arise for one or more of the following general reasons:

1. Competition for scarce resources: A team leader often has to decide how best to allocate scarce resources of time, materials, accommodation and money. Individuals who lose out are likely to be disappointed and if the situation is not handled sensitively by the team leader then there could be bitterness and antagonism. The same situation may arise if two colleagues are competing for the same job.

2. A desire for autonomy: There are still very many teachers who simply want to do 'their own thing' with regard to the children whom they teach. They may publicly subscribe to a collegiate and collaborative approach but will then go off and get on with their own preferred way. If challenged they can become antagonistic and will defend their right to adjust agreed procedures to the specific situation.

3. Divergence over methods and means: Teachers may agree on the fundamental aims of education but disagree strongly on the means of achieving them. They may favour one or another set of teaching materials or methods or one kind of assessment process. They may become quite antagonistic if called upon to adopt approaches they do not like.

4. Personality clashes: Self evidently school teams may comprise a mixture of personalities and as they interact to complete tasks their attitudes to each other can be a source of conflict.

5. Difficult people: Some people are downright difficult in their attitudes to others. They may be competent enough, though sometimes lack of competence is the underlying problem, and yet they can undermine so much effort by their negativity, cynicism and general lack of goodwill and cooperation.

Little surprise then that when school leaders are asked what it is about their job that gives them the greatest amount of stress, they will almost invariably point to relationships with difficult people – be they colleagues, parents or pupils.

Difficult people can severely disrupt the achievement of any school's vision merely by withholding their goodwill and cooperation – especially if they then encourage others to do the same.

Conversely, of course, it is important to remember that many teachers can point to the fact that their leaders are the ones who are difficult people and that it is their unreasonable demands that are the source of stress to them. What makes 'difficult people' situations especially problematic is that quite often the difficult people are not so lacking in competence that they can be removed from their post. Indeed it is notoriously difficult to remove even a quite obviously incompetent teacher.

Difficult people use up enormous amounts of a leader's energy and time, time that is not then available to devote to the support and development of those colleagues who are not difficult. So it is vital for any leader to develop the skills that may help to resolve or reduce conflict and the damage caused by difficult people.

Dealing with conflict and difficult people

The approaches used by a leader to resolve conflict vary as no one style will fit all situations. Research, however, strongly supports the *contingency* approach – diagnosing a conflict to identify the best ways of managing it under the given conditions that provide the context of the conflict. Using this approach, a school leader begins by determining if a conflict really exists. If it does, the conflict should be diagnosed, various management strategies should be reviewed and the strategy that will lead to an effective solution should be selected.

First Steps

In the first step, the leader decides if a conflict really exists. Sometimes different views only seem incompatible and a discussion to clear the air may resolve the situation.

If there clearly is incompatibility however, the leader should seek out the views of all involved and how they feel about the situation.

When individuals are involved in a confrontation, the way they view the situation will determine to a large extent their willingness to find a solution.

In some cases individuals may display cooperative behaviour, indicating the degree to which they are interested in reaching a satisfactory solution with others. In other cases individuals may display uncooperative behaviour, making it clear that they are unwilling to review their stance and compromise. Once the basic attitudes to the confrontation are clear to the leader, then various strategies may be used to solve it.

Applying the Appropriate Management Strategy

After the conflict has been diagnosed, it must be managed. Once again leadership style is important –and in particular the balance between task-focus and people-focus. The following five approaches to dealing with conflict have been identified, contingent upon the attitude that one brings to the issue.

1. **Avoidance**: The leader copes with the conflict by avoiding it completely. The issues are so unimportant that investing the time and resources necessary to resolve the conflict appears unwise. Or the desire for a peaceful coexistence and the avoidance of a hostile aftermath are given priority. There are advantages and disadvantages to using this approach. Although the conflict and the possible hostility that could result are avoided at the present time, the potential for conflict remains and could resurface at any given time. And the leadership of the leader may be at risk as the third party may feel free to oppose the leader at other times.

2. **Smoothing**: This is related to avoidance. The leader has a desire to maintain positive interpersonal relationships. In order to maintain these positive relationships, disagreements and differences of opinions on substantive issues are

143

minimised. If there is strong evidence to suggest that the education of pupils is at risk then avoidance and smoothing are not really options.

3. **Bargaining**: Moderate levels of concern for both task and relationship are displayed. The parties must agree to enter a problem-solving approach. A solution to the conflict is reached and as a result of both parties making concessions. Neither party is a winner, but neither party is a loser. Sometimes, a third party may be called in to serve as a mediator and given the responsibility of providing assurances that everyone is treated fairly and an equitable compromise is reached.

4. **Power struggle**: There is little concern for interpersonal relationships between the parties involved. The major focus is on task accomplishment. Power and force are used to break down the opposition and win, regardless of the consequences to the other party. Leaders, for reasons that are obvious, should try to avoid getting into power struggles. But again, if the education of pupils is suffering – say by ineffective teaching methods that the third party is defending – then as before the leader does not have any option but to refer the matter higher if the matter defies resolution.

5. **Problem solving**: Problem solving is a collaborative approach to managing conflict. Both parties collaborate in an attempt to achieve the best solution to the conflict. The primary concern is accomplishing the task in a manner that is rational and allows a positive climate to be maintained. This is clearly the best approach, but as noted earlier the basic attitude of the people in conflict has to be analysed. Problem solving cannot work unless people are willing to make it work –and that in its turn is likely to depend upon the overall culture, relationships and climate within the team.

This concludes the thought pieces for Session 4(b)

Activity WS4 (b): Managing Difficult People (aspiring to middle management)

Consider the steps that you would have taken as a team leader to deal with a problem like Maria, whose case is described below.

List the following and if possible discuss the case with other colleagues.

(i)	The sources of conflict described above that you were able to identify in the case of Maria
(ii)	Elements in the case that might be characterised as functional and dysfunctional conflict
(iii)	The interpersonal skills that you would need to manage such a conflict successfully
(iv)	The principles that would guide any action you would take to resolve or reduce it.
(v)	The steps you would take to deal with the situation

Not long after Maria joined the school as a surplus teacher from another school, it became clear to her senior colleagues that they had a problem on their hands. It was not so much that Maria lacked a measure of teaching competence, although in truth she was not by any means a wonderful teacher and did not even seem to like children all that much. In her behaviour and in her comments she tended to convey the message that, as a very experienced teacher, she had nothing new to learn. She tended to greet proposals for initiatives with cynical remarks. If children failed to do well in her class then that was clearly the fault of the children themselves, their parents, the nature of the local community and the senior management team. She invariably seemed to adopt a minimalist approach so far as undertaking her duties was concerned and was always first out of the car park. One particular aspect of her approach that caused concern was that she clearly felt that she had the right to disregard agreed procedures whenever it suited her.

On one occasion the head of department responsible for her work found her running a lesson that focused on practising skills that had already been well practised instead of delivering the agreed lesson that focused on new skills. Her explanation was that the children preferred practising the old skills and did not want to practise the new ones. The departmental head suspected laziness on the part of Maria rather than any concern for pupils.

On another occasion she changed the agreed procedures for running an examination, claiming despite all evidence to the contrary from previous occasions that her procedures were more helpful to the children. On yet another occasion the departmental head came across two of Maria's pupils squabbling in the corridor outside her door, despite the fact that school policy was not to put pupils outside the classroom unattended. She explained that she had no choice to put the pupils out as they were being so disruptive and, for health and safety reasons she could not leave a class to deal with them. The pupils insisted that they had actually been talking to each other about the work they were doing but Maria would not listen to their protestations of innocence.

Before long Maria's negative and arbitrary style was causing stress among her other colleagues, and there was evidence to suggest that Maria's pupils were doing less well than others.

Maria's behaviour was not confined to her own situation. On one occasion she got into an argument in the corridor with a colleague about whose turn it was to use an IT facility. And on another occasion she complained loudly in the staffroom about not being given time off to be at home for a visiting Gas Board official. Finally she complained about children's behaviour in several of her classes. No one else was complaining about the behaviour of those same pupils in other classrooms.

Activity WS4 (b): Managing Difficult People (aspiring to senior management)

Consider the steps that you would take if called upon to deal with any of the difficult people in question in the six case studies listed below.

List the following:

  i.   The interpersonal skills that you would need to manage such people successfully

  ii.   The principles that would guide any action you would take

  iii.   The steps you would take to resolve or reduce difficulties

Discuss your list with other colleagues if possible

Case 1:

As depute head, you are linked to a department where the team leader has only a few years to go to retirement. He has been effective in the past but now seems to be happy to delegate, if not abdicate, leadership tasks to younger colleagues who are resentful as they are not being paid for such work.

Case 2:

One of the departments with whom you are linked includes a long-serving teacher who has been passed over for internal promotion, even of an acting kind, and now sees herself being overtaken by younger colleagues. Any time she spoke to the HT she was simply told that the job went to the best applicant and that that was no reflection on her competence or potential. She has recently been applying for posts elsewhere with no success and is becoming more and more bitter as she suspects that senior management are blocking a move.

Case 3:

A particular teacher is forever trying to undermine the authority of the HT and other senior managers by spreading rumour and criticism – but only in informal contexts such as the gossip corner in the staff room. He does not usually express opposition to school policies in public debate but is quick to share with colleagues over coffee the 'real' reason why certain decisions have been made.

Case 4:

A certain teacher is struggling badly with the demands of the job. He is comfortable with small groups such as the after-school cello club that he runs. But he is overwhelmed with discipline problems in larger classes of difficult children. He has been offered the opportunity to attend CPD programmes on managing pupil behaviour but it seems to make no difference. He blames the pupils for his woes and yet other teachers seem to manage fine with the same pupils. The head of department asks you as the link member of the SMT to suggest what should happen next.

Case 5:

An excellent teacher is promoted internally to head of one of your link departments. But it becomes clear fairly soon that whatever his teaching skills may be he is not coping with the demands of his new role of leader and manager. There are suspicions that he is beginning to drink to excess because of the pressures he is under.

Case 6:

The head of the art department, one of your link departments as a DHT, complains to you that a member of the school's pastoral team, who is from the physics department, has used her influence to persuade a bright senior pupil to choose to study 'higher physics' rather than 'higher art', despite the fact that there is every possibility that the pupil could gain an 'A' rating in higher art whereas she is struggling with physics. The head of art had approached the pastoral teacher about the matter and there had been a bit of a fall-out between them with the pastoral teacher angrily declaring that she had simply accommodated the pupil's preferences.

Feedback: Activity WS4(b): A Case Study (middle managers)

Happily, there are not too many 'Marias' in the system. Yet even one can take up endless amounts of time and emotion on the part of the team leader. The critical question has to be the extent to which the negative attitudes of such difficult people have an impact on the education of their pupils. And it must also be remembered that team leaders are operating within an overall system in which dismissal for incompetence is extremely unusual.

Many respondents to the Maria case recognised the need to develop a two-pronged strategy, a *developmental strategy* that seeks every opportunity to engage the commitment and skills of such a teacher and a *damage limitation strategy* that seeks to minimise the negative impact on children of their attitudes.

The 'Maria' in question was a member of the team led by the head of department who featured in *Thought Piece 3.7* in Session 3. She constantly sought to engage Maria in the work of the team and consistently followed up and queried the decisions that she made. Every time she was tempted to avoid yet another example of Maria's destructiveness she would make a point of speaking to her as a priority, providing every opportunity to Maria to explain her position but asserting calmly and clearly what should have happened.

In terms of damage limitation she tried to ensure that she or another reliable colleague would be working adjacent to Maria in open-plan working spaces and opportunities for team-teaching were pursued. Again, Maria would not be allocated the same pupils two years running if it was at all possible. Again, so far as possible, the head of department would not allocate teaching groups preparing for national examinations to Maria or would ensure that such groups would not be taught by Maria every period. She did not, however, want to initiate disciplinary procedures.

Feedback: Activity WS4(b): Six Case Studies (senior managers)

We begin by looking briefly at each of the six case studies in terms of how respondents felt they should be dealt with, although as with all difficult people there are a variety of different responses. Then we look at some recurring points regarding the skills required, the principles to follow and the steps to take when dealing with conflict and difficult people – including the overall two-pronged strategy already described above.

Case 1

The general view is that in the first instance the DHT should establish whether or not the team members have raised their concerns directly with the team leader rather than simply going over his head to complain at a higher level. If not, the DHT should advise them to do so by pointing out their concerns in a diplomatic way to the team leader. It may, for example, be the case that the team leader is deliberately delegating in order to develop the leadership skills of any possible successor.

If team members have already raised their concerns but have gained little by way of response then the DHT should seek an early meeting to discuss the matter with the team leader and to invite his/her comments. The DHT would then remind the team leader of his proven track record and insist that it is essential to maintain that high level of service.

He might point out that the alternative could well be that team members will take out a formal grievance against the team leader and that on the face of things such a grievance would probably be upheld.

Case 2

In case 2, the general view is that the DHT should make it clear that it is not for him or her to judge any allegations. But the DHT should offer to sit down with the teacher, together with the departmental head, and conduct a staff development review meeting, if this has not happened before. It would be important for the DHT and the departmental head to make clear their opinion of the teacher's knowledge, skills and attitudes. Alternatively, the teacher might prefer to speak either to the DHT or departmental head alone.

If the teacher is keen on promotion then the DHT can offer to source appropriate leadership development CPD opportunities. At the same time, the DHT can point out that there is a lot of competition for promotion and many good teachers will not be promoted. But at the very least, following up an appropriate CPD opportunity will help the teacher to do his or her current job more effectively – and should help his or her chances of promotion, even if there are no guarantees. It would be important for the middle and senior managers involved to avoid any ambiguity.

Case 3

It may be a good idea simply not to respond to such gossip and rumour. Like Lord Nelson, there are times when it is good for leaders to decide that they can see no ships. The grapevine is a vital element in the informal structures of any school and can be a good way of allowing people to let off steam. Other colleagues will know fine well what the rumour-monger is up to and he or she will have no success in undermining the authority of senior leaders respected for their integrity.

If the activities of such a colleague are, however, seriously undermining the fundamental purposes of the school then once again it is very much a matter of the relevant senior leader grasping nettles and challenging the colleague in question about his or her purposes. If the colleague has a legitimate grievance then let it be heard in public with suitable supporting evidence. Such grievances should rightly be heard and addressed. But if it is clear that the colleague is simply indulging in destructive behaviour, perhaps as part of a personal vendetta, as a result of being passed over for promotion for example, then the person should be exposed for the disruptive influence that he or she is. Disciplinary action may even be called for, although it is important not to make a martyr out of someone who may not ultimately have all that much influence in the first place.

Case 4

It seems clear that the teacher in question is simply not up to the demands of the job and there may be questions to be asked as to how he or she received a teaching qualification in the first place. A meeting with the teacher should be convened, with the teacher being supported by a trade union or other colleague. It should be made clear to the teacher that there are no winners in the existing situation. The teacher in question is likely to be under considerable stress that will be doing nothing for his or her health, and his or her inability to cope must be having a deleterious effect on pupil performance.

151

There is likely also to be a strain on colleagues who may be called from time to time to cover for the teacher's shortcomings. Clearly it is unlikely to be possible to time table the teacher all the time for small, manageable groups. The teacher should be advised to find another job more suited to his or her skills. Ultimately he or she is liable to be faced with a disciplinary procedure for incompetence.

Case 5

This type of situation needs to be addressed with some urgency. Apart from anything else the teacher needs to be made aware of the concerns about alcohol and needs to be advised of the support mechanisms that are available at school or authority level. At the same time, it may be that the teacher needs CPD in leadership and management and should be offered the opportunity to undertake appropriate developmental activities. Ultimately it may be necessary to advise the teacher to revert to the role of a classroom teacher, for his or her own sake and for the sake of his or her pupils and colleagues.

Case 6

The DHT clearly has to investigate these complaints – but with an open mind. The pupil should be given a full career interview and the implications of the various choices open to her should be made clear to her before she is invited to say which choice she would prefer. In the event it did appear as if there has been some subtle pressure put on the pupil to choose physics and the pastoral teacher was given a 'word to the wise'. The pupil went on to get an 'A' in art – and secured a pass in higher physics in sixth year, where she had more time to focus on the subject.

The general *skills* that researchers mention in connection with managing conflict include the following:

- The essential courage to grasp nettles rather than avoid them
- The ability to focus on policies rather than personalities, issues rather than individuals and ideas rather than irrationality.
- The ability to listen to and seek clarification of the other viewpoint
- The ability to present ideas and feelings, calmly but assertively
- The ability to 'helicopter' above disputes and analyse them
- The ability to find common goals among the differences as the first step in a renewed approach to joint working

- Patience and perseverance

Unsurprisingly this list has much in common with the list of skills required of the good motivator that we discussed earlier and is clearly linked to the communication and decision-making techniques that we discussed in the previous section of this session.

Principles for dealing with conflict include the following:

- Distinguish between functional and dysfunctional conflict.
- Don't confuse conflict with richness in diversity
- Deal with conflict at the earliest possible moment
- More communication is better than less communication
- Talk to your adversary not about them
- Make time to hear your adversary
- Look for opportunities for your adversary to shine
- Avoid win-lose solutions. For people who are trying to build teams they are the same as lose-lose solutions
- Avoid 'reward' situations that do not include your adversary
- Try not to take things personally
- Always remember the value of 'Please' and 'Thank You'
- Be aware of discipline and grievance procedures – just in case

As before, it is not difficult to see the link between such principles and skills and the principles and skills of motivating people. Conflict often comes about precisely because team leaders did not practise motivational skills in the first place or failed to think through the steps that they should take to minimise conflict when it did arise.

Inter-colleague conflict

Our focus so far has been on conflict of a kind that may arise between a leader and a follower. Sometimes, however tensions arise between followers. In such cases, the leader may be invited by one party or another to try and resolve the situation – or may decide to intervene anyway. Case study 6 above has elements of such a situation.

Such intervention runs the risk of exacerbating the situation rather than resolving it. The best a leader can do is to recommend to the parties involved that they discuss the matter between themselves. Certainly the leader should be available in reserve to assist if both parties are happy about that. But the leader may have to be available to deal with a grievance by one colleague against another and it is unwise to cloud the issue by overhasty intervention which then may be perceived as the leader taking sides – always a lose/lose situation!

If it becomes clear that any conflict is heading towards disciplinary or grievance procedures – and this possibility might become clear quite early on – then a team leader should alert the head teacher accordingly.

It is arguable that the head of department who worked so hard and so long to engage the commitment of the intransigent Maria in the case study for middle managers described above should have asked for formal assistance at an earlier stage once she had exhausted all avenues of support. And the DHT in case study 6 rightly intervened quickly to ensure that the pupil was not a victim of interpersonal dispute among colleagues.

Conflict is one thing and incompetence is another – although they are often connected. Hence the need ultimately for an awareness of due procedures and the formal recording of events, time-consuming and emotion-consuming though this may be. It is not for the team leader to conduct grievance or disciplinary hearings, but it is certainly important that the team leader should have done everything possible to support a colleague and retained a record of that – just in case things come to the worst and formal procedures have to be initiated.

Workshop Session 5: Planning Improvement

Workshop Session 5: Planning Improvement

Introduction

The four workshop sessions presented so far are concerned with awareness-raising of some of the key functions and qualities demanded of excellent team leaders. But as has already been noted, leadership is best developed by practising it.

This workshop is related to the second element of this overall programme – the drawing up an improvement plan which then will be implemented over a school session under the leadership of the reader or course participant.

The concept of improvement is addressed in two senses. In one sense , it is about improving some aspect of school provision in such a way that pupil performance will be raised; in the second sense, improvement relates to development of the leadership skills of the person leading the school-based project.

Accordingly, planning improvement involves two preliminary elements:

- Drawing up an action plan that will direct the school-based project

- Drawing up a personal learning plan that will direct leadership development

Leadership of such a project will need to be negotiated with the head teacher within the context of the school's improvement plan as it will need staff volunteers to join the project team and appropriate support from senior management with regard to various resources, not least time.

This workshop provides an opportunity for readers to practise drawing up the two elements of an improvement plan – an action plan and a personal learning plan.

The management process and the planning process

For the purposes of this programme we focus on a *management process* and on a set of *planning* procedures that should be taken by readers as part of their intention to lead a school-based project.

It is particularly important for any team leader to appreciate that effective planning, especially in terms of *action planning*, is one of the best ways of securing the commitment of individual colleagues, of motivating them and of building team spirit.

Indeed, it has been argued that effective leadership and management is essentially the same thing as effective planning and implementing of change because it is in times of change that the abilities of a leader are most severely put to the test. We may see the validity of this link by comparing what has become known as the *management process* with what has become known as the *planning process*.

The management process

There are four stages in the *management process:*

Audit: at this stage the manager leads analysis of the current situation to identify strengths and areas for development. This leads to identification of priorities for development for which plans need to be prepared

Plan: at this stage the manager leads the design of a detailed plan of the action that is to be taken if the priority development is to be achieved, in discussion with the colleagues who will help to implement the plan.

Implement: at this stage plans are put into effect as agreed. This stage includes the process of monitoring to ensure that agreed arrangements are being effected.

Evaluate: at this stage the impact of the proposed changes is evaluated. In the case of education, evaluation of impact is especially concerned with impact on learning and teaching and pupil attainment and achievement.

This APIE *management process* is a recurring process. At the same time, what we call the *planning process* features the same four recurring steps. This is hardly surprising as leadership and management skills are most obviously called into play in times of change, as we have already noted. Both processes are concerned with translating the values, vision and aims of a school, or an individual, into reality.

There is also a degree of similarity between the management and planning processes and the *experiential learning* process described in *Thought Piece A.* They are all concerned with the process of reviewing current events, thinking about and planning new approaches, putting these new approaches into practice and evaluating outcomes before moving on to the next stage of the journey– although sequencing may seldom be quite as orderly as that. Tracking back and forward is common and indeed planning can sometimes feel as if it is all about one step forward and two back. Nevertheless the management or planning process will always be at one or other of the four stages described.

Learning Outcomes

By the end of this session you will have:

- ✓ Understood the connection between the management process and the planning process
- ✓ Written a draft action plan with rationale
- ✓ Reflected upon your overall planning skills

Session 5: Planning Improvement

Thought Piece 5.1: Planning and school improvement

There are three issues from the literature on planned change that are crucial to our formulation of school improvement strategies. These three issues relate to the unfolding of the change process over time, the importance of student outcomes and the meaning individuals make of the change process.

The first issue is the way in which the change process unfolds. It is not linear but consists of a series of three stages that merge into each other. Although in practice these stages often co-exist, there is some advantage in describing them separately, particularly in terms of what happens during them, and what behaviours during each phase make for success. The process is usually considered to consist of three overlapping phases: *initiation, implementation and institutionalisation.*

The *initiation* phase is about deciding to embark on innovation and developing commitment towards the process. The key activities in the initiation phase are the decision to begin innovation and a review of the current state of affairs in the area of provision that is in focus. There are, however, a number of factors associated with initiation that will influence whether the change gets off to a good start in the first place. Much will depend on existing attitudes to change within the departmental team and

the availability of resources to support the proposed change. It is also important that the innovation should relate to a local agenda and a local need. Where a priority is imposed from outside the school, then at the very least the individual department or working group should be free to address it in a way that reflects the current state of readiness of the working group in question. If, for example, an authority decides that there should be a special focus on formative assessment, and a given department in a school is already a leader in formative assessment processes, then clearly such a department should be free to focus on other priorities. The success of the initiation phase also requires a clear and well-structured approach to initial planning and the clear commitment of the group leader to the change in question.

In this connection, it may well be that a bit of top-down pushing from the leader is in order to get the initiative moving at the start. If, however, no amount of pushing succeeds in gaining at least the initial willingness of colleagues to engage then it may be that the initiative has to be abandoned. If you are in a hole, stop digging.

Implementation is of course the phase where the action begins. It is during this phase that skills and understanding are being acquired, some success is hopefully being achieved and responsibility for particular activities is shared by members of the team. The key activities occurring during implementation are the carrying out of action plans, the developing and sustaining of commitment, the checking of progress and the overcoming of problems.

Research indicates that the key factors for success at this stage include clear coordination by the team leader, shared control over implementation (*not* top-down pushing this time), an insistence on 'doing it right' balanced by due resource support, adequate and sustained opportunities for CPD and rewards for teachers early in the process, not only in terms of empowerment and due praise but also in providing some valuable time as necessary.

If for some reason it is not possible to support implementation in the above ways then it may be that plans and targets will have to be adjusted accordingly if any momentum is to be maintained. Again, do not dig beyond the possible.

Institutionalisation is the phase where innovation and change stop being regarded as something new and become part of the school's usual way of doing things. There has been a tendency in the past to assume that this stage happened automatically. This is despite the evidence that some innovations fade away after an initial wave of enthusiasm, or after an important contributor leaves or when funding and other resources cease.

The move from implementation to institutionalisation, however, often involves rolling out a small pilot project, often without the advantage of previously available funding. Indeed it is worth keeping in mind when planning a pilot project that there is not much point in promoting practices that simply cannot be sustained on a larger scale. But so long as all is well, widespread use of the change will become common among staff and its impact will be progressively seen on classroom practice.

Key activities at this stage are: an emphasis on embedding the change within the department's structures; the elimination of contradictory practices; and clear links to other change efforts and to what is happening in the classroom. The failure of many efforts towards change to progress beyond early implementation is partially explained by the lack of realisation on the part of those involved that the above activities are necessary. They have also failed to realise that each phase has different characteristics that need different strategies if success is to be achieved.

The second issue in planned change is the importance of process leading to outcomes. The logic of the approach is as follows: we begin with some educational goal, which leads to some form of innovation. The impact and outcomes of the innovation are dependent on the nature of the initiation decisions (both within and outside the school), the factors affecting implementation, the implementation strategy and the degree to which institutionalisation is achieved – all of which are embedded in, and dependent upon, the culture of the school. The important point is that all of this effort should have some impact on pupil learning. Despite the evident truth of this point it is one that is unfortunately neglected in many change efforts where there is little evaluation. We shall return to this topic in the *Session 6* workshop.

The third issue relates to the meaning that individuals give to their involvement in the change process. As Michael Fullan, a guru of change forces points out, real change, whether desired or not, represents 'a serious and collective experience characterised by ambivalence and uncertainty' for the individual involved. For some, the experience of change is individually threatening and disconcerting. If the result of this engagement is to be empowerment and fulfilment, then such a judgement can only be made with hindsight. There is no certainty as one works through the process of change that meaning will be achieved.

To sum up, it must be remembered that there are various implications when individuals are asked to alter their ways of thinking and doing:

- Change takes place over time
- Change initially involves anxiety and uncertainty

161

- Technical and psychological support is crucial
- The learning of new skills is incremental and developmental
- Organisational conditions within the school or department make it more or less likely that improvement will occur
- Successful change involves a mixture of challenge and support within a collaborative setting

(Adapted from David Hopkins, 1997)

4.2: Attitudes to planning:

The following accounts (apart from Michael Fullan's) are fictitious in as much as no single person said all of these things. But the sentiments sum up what different people have said. To that extent they provide genuine perspectives on the value of planning:

Jo

There is no point in writing a DP. It has no useful purpose. It is merely an administrative task – a complete waste of time. The only function is to keep those above you off our backs and it keeps the LEA happy. We cannot plan in our department because there are lots of factors beyond our control. Things keep changing so rapidly, I don't even know who is in my department next year. Most of the time, the priorities are someone else's priorities and not ours. I write the DP for the few departmental priorities that we are allowed, based upon what I know. It's intuitive. No one in the department is interested and they don't want any CPD. They need all their time to do the job of teaching.

Joanne

I have found writing the DP a very useful exercise. It has helped me to clarify my thoughts and to set targets and goals that are attainable. I have been able to establish my priorities for the future. I try to involve as many people as possible so that all of my department know what needs to be done, where we are going and why. Some of the department draft bits of the DP and we all get together to amend the drafts before I put it all together. I speak to every member of the department about their individual CPD plans for the future year. DP writing provides a good opportunity to put together fresh ideas. On the other hand we are able to plan something that is really manageable. I use the DP as a checklist of events and activities and it keeps us on track for the rest of the year. We are able to monitor and review our progress. When thing don't go right, we can reflect upon why and avoid making the same mistakes again.

(Leask and Terrell. 1997)

Michael Fullan, change guru, expresses his attitude to planning

'The emphasis should be on doing rather than elaborate planning. In a recent study, a researcher found that the size of the planning document was inversely related to the amount and quality of implementation. As the researcher concluded, 'the prettiness of the plan was inversely (or perhaps we should say perversely!) related to student achievement'. This is not a message that says abandon all planning. It means reduce the distance between planning and action. Put another way, the planning is built into the doing, feedback and corrective action. Written plans should be brief and geared to action, monitoring, and rapid feedback and focused instructional improvement, including teachers learning from each other.'

Michael Fullan (2006) 'Turnaround Leadership', Jossey- Bass

This completes the thought pieces for Workshop Session 5.

.

Activity WS5(1): Planning Improvement: The action plan

Individually, draw up a draft *action plan* for the proposed school-based improvement project that you hope to lead as part of your involvement in this leadership development programme. In due course you will be presenting the plan to the colleagues with whom you hope to implement the plan.

The draft plan may represent your *actual* intentions or it may be drawn up purely for the purpose of *practising* your planning skills. Either way, you should draw up the draft plan using the layout provided in the pages that follow. Notes of guidance on completion and a completed sample action plan are part of the information that follows.

Alternatively, you may use action planning forms of a type that are already favoured in your own school, so long as these school versions cover the same requirements as the forms provided here.

Prepare copies of your draft plan and find an opportunity to discuss it with colleagues before drawing up a final version.

Readers are invited to email their draft plans to the programme writer if they wish to have expert formative assessment of their efforts. (See the preface for details)

The personal learning plan

Follow up your action plan with a personal learning plan in which you indicate the functions and qualities that you intend to develop as part of your leadership of the school-based project.

As with the action plan, you may find helpful the notes for guidance that follow, together with the sample personal learning plan.

As with the action plan, readers who email their personal learning plans to the programme writer will receive expert formative assessment of their efforts.

Developing Excellent Team Leaders

Guidance in Completing Development Plans

(a) The Project Action Plan

Contact details: Name, address, telephone, email address (both home and school)

Project Objective:

Overall you want to be as **specific** as you can be in your planning. Researchers speak of *SMART* plans. They are: Specific; Measurable; Achievable; Realistic; Timed. Try to express project objectives in terms of outcomes for pupils that will be demonstrable and if possible measurable. Distinguish between means and ends in your thinking. Thus agreeing a policy statement or developing new materials or trying out some new method of teaching or assessment will be part of your implementation strategy for improving pupil performance rather than objectives in themselves. Process is important, however, so you may want to express your project objectives as outcomes for pupils that come about because of certain strategies. Examples: To implement the AiFL initiative in writing to improve performance levels among P4 – P7 children; to introduce new methods and materials in S5 that will help to take SQA attainment to a given level in a given subject; to reduce referrals for disruptive behaviour among a given cohort by agreeing and implementing a new behaviour policy.

Project Rationale:

Why are you undertaking this particular project? Why is it such a priority? What evidence do you have to support your concerns and where did it come from? What is the baseline from which you need to progress and that you will later be using as a yardstick to measure progress? Try again to be as specific as possible. 100-150 words should probably be enough**.** *How* you intend to go about things should be included in the *implementation strategy* section of the action plan (See below)

Success Criteria:

 In essence, what is it that will satisfy you that your project has achieved its objectives? The more precise your objectives, the more your success criteria will tend to be those same objectives expressed as outcomes. Your success criteria are likely to reflect (a) in the short term your desire to introduce new teaching methods and/or materials (b) in the mid term what you hope to achieve in terms of improved classroom practice and above all (c) in the long term what you hope to achieve in terms of improved achievement and attainment by pupils as a result of the project.

Implementation Strategies

In essence this is likely to be expressed in terms of the APIE management process that was described earlier in Session 4. Describe how you intend to *audit* the existing state of affairs. Describe stages in your *planning* process in terms of agreeing policy, choosing or creating new materials, agreeing new methods. Explain how you intend to pilot or otherwise *implement* your new approaches over time. Note that *Completion dates and Personnel Involved* provide you with the opportunity to give details of these aspects of the strategy. The *monitoring and evaluation* stage of the management process is dealt with in the sections below.

Completion Dates

Specify the due dates by which you hope to have reached certain milestones in your overall implementation strategy

Personnel Involved

Apart from yourself as project leader, who else will be working with you in order to achieve your objectives?

Resource Requirements

Try to be as specific here as possible. For example, state that you will need six one-hour meetings of your project group rather than 'time'. Quantify any money or materials that you might need. What CPD, apart from that which will accrue from membership of your working group, will any of the group members need?

This is not a wish list. You should negotiate these details with the HT or senior colleague. New project leaders find it difficult to estimate resource requirements – and typically underestimate – but the more they try the better they become at estimating such needs. And Head Teachers certainly appreciate carefully costed bids for support as they seek to make wisest use of resources for promoting school improvement initiatives

Methods of monitoring:

What steps will you take to ensure that agreed procedures are carried out? Will you visit classrooms? Will you seek written or verbal reports? Will part of meeting agendas include a progress report section?

Methods of evaluation:

What methods and tools will you use to evaluate impact on teaching, learning and attainment? Classroom visits, questionnaires, quality indicators, attainment statistics in school and national examinations and discussions with staff, pupils and parents are likely to figure here.

(b) The Personal Learning Plan

Professional actions: I intend to:

Identify the key actions that you intend to undertake as you lead your colleagues through the various stages of the unfolding project. These are likely to be linked to the implementation strategies in your action plan.

Professional values: I shall demonstrate my commitment to:

Indicate the particular commitments that you expect to demonstrate as you undertake the project. These are likely to derive from the self-evaluation that you undertook in Session1 of the input days, using the values listed in the Standard for Team Leadership

Personal qualities and interpersonal skills: I intend to improve my ability to:

Focus on key interpersonal skills that you feel you need to work on. These are likely to be based, as with other permeating elements, on the self-evaluation that you carried out during Session 1 of the programme input days.

Knowledge and understanding: I intend to find out more about:

Specify aspects of knowledge and information that relate to your particular project that you wish to gain. There are also areas of knowledge and understanding relating to certain leadership skills that you will wish to know more about. Again, your self-evaluation will guide you here.

Background reading: I intend to read:

It may be difficult for you to specify texts in advance but wherever possible indicate the books you hope to read or the chapters within the books. Background readings and the bibliography given to you during the input days should give you an idea of what you are likely to read, especially with regard to leadership skills. No doubt there will be other texts that are specific to your chosen project.

Sources of support: I intend to seek the support of:

Indicate the people whom you expect to approach for assistance in completing your project.

Recording Progress and Impact

Indicate the methods you will use to keep a record and evidence of your unfolding project and of its ongoing impact on learning, teaching and attainment.

Developing Excellent Team Leaders: Sample Sections of Action Plan

Contact details: as provided

Project Objective

I intend to involve P4 – P7 pupils in the process of personal learning planning (PLP) as one way of helping them to improve attainment and/or achievement in maths and language and behaviour.

Project Rationale:

Last session, in my role as a PT in primary school I was responsible for leading the whole staff in embedding formative assessment in every class. We agreed to use the same strategies in all classes for story writing and teachers could also develop strategies in other curricular areas where they felt it was appropriate and manageable. The plan went well. Children became more focused on their work and more enthusiastic about story writing, the quality of which improved accordingly.

Building on this, several teachers now feel ready to be involved in a pilot project to develop personal learning planning with pupils in their classes. Next session all pupils in P4 – P7 will be involved. We also want to involve parents so at a parents' night in June I gave parents the opportunity to discuss issues with me. They were also given a booklet containing information about AiFL. We plan to encourage pupils to focus on a maximum of 3 targets at any one time – one from personal and social development and two from any curricular area. On the basis of previous experience with formative learning I believe that we can improve behaviour and motivation initially and that we can raise attainment in the longer term. I would also like to make links with A Curriculum for Excellence by encouraging children to develop a folio which will contain children's PLPS and evidence of their wider achievements in order to encourage them to become not only successful learners but also confident individuals, effective contributors and responsible citizens.

Success Criteria:

Ultimately I want to raise pupil attainment in the areas they specify but along the way I want to have improved: teacher teamwork; teaching methods by embedding formative assessment strategies within lessons; the confidence of pupils in planning and evaluating their own learning and the development of folios for recording pupil achievements

Sample Sections of Action Plan Continued

TABLE NOT PROPERLY SUBMITTED - PLEASE RESUBMIT

Methods of monitoring:

I shall attend all meetings and have frequent discussion with colleagues regarding progress in implementation. I shall visit classes to observe work and provide support for colleagues as required. I shall video discussions with pupils and then discuss these with colleagues

Methods of Evaluation:

I shall invite pupils and parents to complete a pre- and post project questionnaire regarding effectiveness; pupil attainments in maths and language will be recorded immediately before and after the project and analysed. I will use Quality Indicators from HGIOS and the AiFL Toolkit before and after the project focusing on QIs 1.1, 2.1, 5.3 and 5.9

Sample of Completed Personal Learning Plan

Professional Actions: I intend to:

- Draw up a plan to develop personal learning planning
- Organise and chair a number of meetings of a development group
- Revise existing teaching methods to improve pace and challenge for all pupils
- Evaluate the working of the group and make recommendations

Professional Values: I shall demonstrate my commitment to:

- Effective learning and teaching for all
- The importance of encouraging children to recognise their personal strengths and needs and to plan next steps
- Developing the confidence of children to enable them to seek help to achieve their goals
- My personal development and the development of others

Personal Qualities and Interpersonal Skills: I wish to develop my ability to:

- Be more confident
- Inspire and motivate others
- Build an effective team
- Communicate more effectively

Knowledge and Understanding: I want to find out more about:

- The principles of managing change
- The characteristics an effective team
- The use of QIs to evaluate impact in the classroom
- The use of Assessment for learning strategies to improve learning and attainment

Background Reading: I intend to read:

All background articles dealing with session issues; relevant AiFL material; HGIOS: Journey to Excellence; relevant chapters from books included in the core reading list on such topics as communication, motivation and team-building

Sources of Support: I intend to seek the support of:

My HT; Course tutor; local authority personnel; LTScotland consultants; colleagues working on similar projects

Recording of Progress/Impact:

I intend to keep minutes of meetings, copies of questionnaires, notes of discussions, comments on the value of CPD, evidence of pupil work, relevant performance statistics.

Submission date: as provided

Activity WS5(2) Action plan presentations

If it is at all possible, share your draft plan with colleagues who you hope will participate in implementation and invite formative comment from them, using the form that is presented on the next page. Clarify that your head teacher is willing to endorse and support your proposal.

In the case of input days that are run centrally, groups of three participants will each provide their group colleagues in rotation with a presentation on their thinking behind the draft plan they have drawn up and the leadership skills they hope to develop. They should prepare a 10-minute presentation in total on their action plan and their personal learning plan. Then colleagues will assess the clarity of their planning for for a further 10 minutes before providing 5 minutes of feedback, using for both purposes the formative assessment forms that are provided below.

It is essential that all times should be strictly adhered to. In total, 75 minutes are available for this activity with a maximum of 25 minutes devoted in total to each presentation, including questioning and feedback.

Three roles are envisaged:

A: The presenter

B: The chairperson

C: The critical friend

A: The *presenter* will present his/her plans and explain the thinking behind them

B: The *chairperson* will make sure timings are adhered to and prepare feedback notes

C: The *critical friend* will lead the probing of the draft plans, assisted by the chairperson

Each member of the triad will play each role in rotation.

Assessing Plans: The Action Plan

In assessing the quality of draft plans, assessors should consider:

Clarity of rationale:

- Is there a clear description of the baseline situation that needs to be improved and why?
- Is there a clear description of the audit processes and tools used to identify the baseline situation?
- Do success criteria specify desired outcomes in terms of improvements in the original baseline situation.

Clarity and validity of objective and success criteria:

- The project objective follows logically from the rationale
- The project objective is learning-focused
- Success criteria specify desired outcomes in terms of improvements in the original baseline situation.

Clarity of overall implementation strategies

Are proposals clear in terms of:

- The people to be involved
- The timescale
- The meetings to be held
- The implications for material, financial and time resources
- The implications for staff development
- Arrangements for monitoring the implementation of the plan
- Methods of and instruments for the evaluation of the impact on learning and teaching

Assessing Plans: The Personal Learning Plan

In assessing the quality of personal learning plans, assessors should consider the following:

Professional actions:

Are proposed actions clear and manageable in number?

Professional values:

Are statements about specific commitments clearly expressed?

Personal qualities and interpersonal skills:

Are the qualities and skills to be developed clearly defined? Is it likely that implementation of the declared plan will provide opportunities for qualities and skills to be developed.

Knowledge and understanding:

Are specific kinds of knowledge and understanding to be developed clearly described – both in terms of specific knowledge and understanding that relates to the project in question and in terms of generic principles of leadership and management?

Background reading:

Is proposed background reading clearly specified, both with regard to texts that relate to leadership and management and to texts that relate to the project in question?

Sources of support:

Is the range of personnel to be consulted clear? If the participant intends to follow up other development programmes, has this been made clear?

Recording Progress and Impact

The final stage in the overall development programme involves participants in writing a reflective report on how well they led a school-based project team and an analysis of its impact, both with regard to pupil development and with regard to personal leadership development

Accordingly, does the personal learning plan make it clear how the aspiring leader will keep a record of the unfolding project and of its ongoing impact on learning, teaching, attainment and personal leadership development?

Feedback Session WS5(1) and WS5(2): Action Plan Presentations

The quality of planning varies according to experience. Typically, early efforts at planning tend to feature (a) taking on too big a project (b) serious underestimation of workload factors, not least time (c) an inability to cost the various stages of the initiative sensibly (d) failure to include variables that, with hindsight, seem obvious.

There is too a tendency, especially in implementation, to try and do everything personally instead of treating the concept of distributed leadership with due seriousness. Previous participants have frequently admitted not wanting to ask busy colleagues to devote time and energy to *their* project. But it is not *their* project. It is a *school* project that they are leading and which, properly led, will bring benefits to all in terms of better learning, teaching and attainment.

Some participants have found it useful to use a *SWOT* analysis with their colleagues to work through the strengths, weaknesses, opportunities and threats that may impact on achieving their objectives.

Some also think through their draft plans by subjecting them to a *TIPS* process: *Thinking/Intentions/Problems/Solutions*. This involves them in thinking about their plans and about how they might avoid, or at least minimise, problems.

The procedure is simple enough. Readers draw up a simple chart of four columns, headed – Thinking, Intentions, Problems and Solutions. In the *'Thinking'* column they briefly note what their underlying thinking was for a proposed strategy. In the *'Intentions'* column they note down the specific activities that they intended to undertake as part of their proposed implementation strategy. In the *'Problems'* column, they note down the problems that perhaps arose to thwart their intentions. Finally in the *'Solutions'* column they note down the steps they might need to take in order to get round the problems.

To take an obvious example, a leader might well think that it is important to have meeting times that suit all members of the team and will plan accordingly. In the event, it may not always be possible to have a planned meeting because of some problem that arises. So the leader will want to consider alternative times or ways of making sure that every one can be consulted about any given proposal.

It may even be that original plans for meetings were unrealistic and will have to be adjusted accordingly. Planning skills improve with practice, together with the ability to move from vision to reality.

Workshop Session 6: Improving Outcomes for Learners through Self-evaluation

Workshop Session 6: Improving Outcomes for Learners through Self-evaluation

Introduction

Unlike the other sessions, this one is undertaken by readers as part of their implementation of a school-based project. Indeed ongoing monitoring and evaluation of progress should be built in as part of the implementation process and not bolted on at the end as an afterthought.

Glance through almost any school inspection report and there is a good chance that one of the areas for improvement is the quality of monitoring and evaluation. Teachers devote considerable amounts of time to planning and implementing all sorts of initiatives but are less rigorous in ensuring that the procedures being implemented are in accordance with whatever was agreed and in judging the impact of these new procedures on learners' experiences and learning outcomes.

Partially the problem is that monitoring and evaluating are potentially difficult, sensitive and time - consuming processes. Yet without some evaluation it is impossible to be sure about the differences that have been made — or indeed even if any differences have been made. Accordingly it is almost impossible to be sure about what to do next, if aspects of progress are to be built upon.

The same kind of problem applies to improving leadership. Leadership does not exist in a vacuum. It has no meaning unless there are followers. And so it is essential to go beyond improved knowledge and understanding of the demands of leadership to look at how leadership is working in practice in the same way that it is important to go beyond learning and teaching theory to look at how this is being applied in the classroom.

Leadership Development and Improvement
The basic premise of this programme is that effective leadership contributes to pupil learning; and as leadership skills are developed so pupil learning and attainment may indirectly be raised. We have already looked in Session 1 at what leaders do and what leaders are like. Now we look at the process whereby leadership development promotes school improvement. The process comprises three essential stages:
- ✓ Identifying Needs
- ✓ Meeting Needs
- ✓ Evaluating Impact

All three stages, including evaluation of impact, must be followed through in an ongoing way to maximise the chances of personal and school improvement.

Identifying Needs

The first step is for the aspiring leader to identify what his or her needs are – and at this stage of the programme it would be wise for an aspiring leader once again to conduct a rigorous self-evaluation of his or her current levels of expertise in terms of the *Standard for Team Leadership,* following the initial self-evaluation during workshop Session 1.

Meeting Needs

It is to be hoped that by working through this set of workshops, the aspiring leader will have at least begun the process of further developing current knowledge and understanding about the demands of leadership. Thereafter leadership of the school-based project will offer many opportunities for further development of the values and skills that have been highlighted in the workshop sessions.

Evaluating Impact

Mere improvement in knowledge and understanding of the values, skills and information that the excellent team leader needs will not of itself improve leadership competence. Enhanced understanding of the requirements has to be put to the test. Improved leadership is revealed above all in improved followership and consequential improved pupil performance. Has the improving leader become more effective at selecting colleagues? Has the leader become more effective at developing colleagues? Has the leader become more effective at harnessing the range of skills among colleagues into a team approach? And above all, have all these efforts led to a better quality of teaching in the classroom, leading to a better quality of pupil learning?

In this session we look at:

1. Evaluating your levels of increased awareness and understanding of key elements of leadership and management as a result of undertaking the workshop activities. To what extent have the various learning outcomes of each input session been relevant to your short and long-term development needs?

2. Evaluating the quality of your planning skills as evidenced in your project plans

3. Evaluating in due course the impact that leading a project has had on your leadership values skills and on the development of your colleagues

181

4. Evaluating in due course also the impact of your project on learning and teaching and hence pupil attainment and achievement

Evaluating the workshop input will be overtaken at the end of this workshop session and 2 will be attended to when project plans are submitted for formative assessment. We focus on 3 and 4 in a separate guide to writing an end-of project reflective portfolio. In the meantime we begin by considering the pros and cons of different methods of evaluation, especially with regard to the evaluation of adult performance.

Who should evaluate and how?

In general terms we can distinguish between *external* evaluation (by inspectors and the like), *internal* evaluation (by senior colleagues or for that matter by peers or even junior colleagues – including pupils and their parents) and *self* –evaluation by the individual or a team. In the case of evaluation by others, as opposed to self-evaluation, three kinds of evaluation process, or 'triangulation', are usually utilised relating both to processes and outcomes:

1. Observation of the teacher at work

2. Discussion of issues with the teacher and any senior colleagues who may have responsibility for supporting the teacher

3. Analysis of data pertaining to the performance of pupils taught by the colleague

Learning Outcomes

By the end of this session, you will have:

- ✓ Reviewed the importance of evaluation to professional practice
- ✓ Reflected upon the pros and cons of different methods of evaluation
- ✓ Confirmed the importance of rigorous self-evaluation

Session 6: Improving Outcomes for Learning

Thought Piece 6.1: A cycle for monitoring and evaluating

A cycle for monitoring and evaluating aspects of an improvement initiative in a school can be represented as a series of steps, linked to the planning process itself. The steps will include the need to:

- ✓ Identify the requirement for new activity

- ✓ Design the activity, its targets and desired outcomes

- ✓ Decide on monitoring methods and review dates

- ✓ Allocate necessary resources

- ✓ Carry out the new activity

- ✓ Collect data on targets and objectives as agreed

- ✓ Evaluate progress against targets and objectives

- ✓ Review and report on activity in the light of evaluation

- ✓ Identify the requirement for the next new activity

There are two striking features in this series of steps. One is the very early introduction of planned monitoring arrangements. Too often such arrangements are tagged on at the end of a planning or evaluation process – sometimes even to the surprise of participants. Another striking feature of the cycle is the distance between the 'identify need' and 'carry out activity'. If the curriculum or leadership activity is to be properly monitored and evaluated, then its design and purpose must be clear, and all involved must know both what its targets and its outcomes are, and how they are to be measured within what time frame. The 'necessary resources' may include time and staffing for the monitoring activities to take place, access to administrative support for data analysis, and time for staff to meet and evaluate the activity. The evaluation process may not only assess the activity against the original targets and outcomes, but may also consider whether policies and practices need to be changed and new objectives set.

The cycle can be used to evaluate innovations, both in curriculum content – for example where a new course is to be piloted and evaluated and in curriculum delivery, evaluating new learning and teaching methods for an existing course. It can also be used to evaluate new leadership learning. Where innovations are concerned, it is important to have comparative data to use as benchmarks to evaluate success.

Adapted from: Briggs, Ann. (2002) *Monitoring and Evaluating Learning* in Bush, T and Bell, J. (eds) The Principles and Practice of Educational Management, London: Paul Chapman

6.2: The Impact on Learning of New Leadership Situations

Talking about cycles, we return to the last part of *Thought Piece A* for our final thought piece. Evaluation of the benefits of any CPD development opportunity tends to consist of a fairly hasty ticking of a few boxes in a questionnaire that seeks opinions of the quality of the CPD event. Certainly the input sessions of a CPD programme should be useful as a starter for the process of development. But, as *Thought Piece A* makes clear, leadership development is likely to be a slow and steady process. There are no quick fixes.

Probably the most widely used and popular model for the evaluation of CPD and consequential learning is the one developed by Donald L. Kirkpatrick as long ago as 1959 and most recently redefined and updated in his 1998 book, 'Evaluating Training: the Four Levels.'

The four levels of Kirkpatrick's evaluation model essentially measure:

- Reaction of participants – what they thought of the CPD input

- Learning – the resulting increase for the participant in knowledge and understanding

- Behaviour – the extent to which new knowledge and understanding led to new behaviour

- Impact – the effect of the new behaviour on provision

All of these measures are recommended for a full and meaningful evaluation of learning in organisations. We can see how these levels may be applied to school leadership CPD. And there are clear connections between these levels of evaluation and the points made in the final section of *Thought Piece A*. Accordingly to complete this series of thought pieces, we include below once more that final section.

'The cycle of learning is not complete – indeed it is a more like a continuing spiral rather than a cycle – until you have had an opportunity to evaluate in a rigorous way the impact of your plans, both in terms of pupil performance and leadership development in a new leadership situation, using your experiences in the previous situation as a baseline from which to assess development.

Remarkably, thorough evaluation of progress is often neglected – if HMIE reports on schools are anything to go by. If one hopes to develop as a leader, a series of questions have to be continually asked – and continually answered:

- What new leadership knowledge have I gained so far?

- How has it improved my understanding of the concept of leadership?

- How have my leadership values changed?

- How have my leadership skills improved?

- What influence have I had on the values and skills of the teachers I lead?

- What have I done to help them improve their classroom performance?

- What has been the impact of all this on pupil attainment and achievement?

- What evidence do I have to support my answers to these questions?

Unsurprisingly, it becomes clear that leadership development depends upon an ongoing mixture of practice and reflection upon practice, with the developing leader asking her or himself the same kind of questions over and over again, being willing to consult a range of sources for possible answers and then using the answers to influence practice.'

This completes the thought pieces for Session 6 and also the whole programme. See, however, the bibliography later.

Activity WS6(a): Who should evaluate?

Discuss with your project team colleagues what you see as being the pros and cons of (i) external evaluation (inspection) (ii) internal evaluation by others, (iii) self-evaluation. List key points on a flip chart and try to reach agreement with your team.

Activity WS6(b): How to evaluate

Discuss with your project team what you see as being the pros and cons of (i) observation of the colleague at work, (ii) discussion of issues with a senior colleague (iii) analysis of data pertaining to the attainment and achievements of pupils List key points on a flip chart and try to reach agreement with your team.

Feedback: Activity WS6(a): Who should evaluate?

You have probably found that your discussions reflected the views of what one researcher has called the 'doves' and the 'hawks' in the field of school improvement. The doves argue that if there is to be real change then schools themselves must 'own' their evaluation processes. Otherwise changes will be superficial. The hawks see self-evaluation as a soft option. Unless there is a hard edge to evaluation from outside, difficult issues will be avoided or fudged.

The doves are concerned with 'improving' (the developmental dimension of evaluation) while the hawks seem only concerned with 'proving'. (the accountability dimension) The hawks will point to cases of improvement thanks to external inspection. The doves complain that inspections are extremely stressful and at best can only provide a snapshot of a moment in time, ending up with a picture that does not necessarily reflect the norm. The hawks point to the fact that an experienced inspector can sum up what is happening in a school very quickly and can make valid comparisons with what is happening elsewhere.

The doves point out that what is happening elsewhere may not be relevant and that it is necessary to serve in a school for some time before the impact of local factors can be fully appreciated.

The simple answer is of course that all three forms of evaluation are important. It is arguable that issues of ownership and empowerment would seem to indicate that progress can only ultimately be achieved through self-evaluation. We remember again Fullan's comment that change cannot be mandated. But inspectors, local authority officials and the like have a critical role to play in ensuring that the self-evaluation in question is suitably rigorous. And, as has been noted already, self-evaluation that does not take into consideration to the views of others may become self-delusion. In this connection, it is important to note the new approach to inspection in Scottish schools, launched in September 2008, whereby HMI will engage with school staffs to find out how the results of self-evaluation have brought about improvement (*Improving Outcomes for Learners through Self- evaluation, HMIE, 2008)*

On the other hand, there is an ongoing debate about quality *control* (after-the-event inspection) and quality *assurance* (planning before and during the event to get it right first time) Inspection tends to be a post-hoc analysis of what happened so that improvements may be made in the future. This may be all very well for the next generation of students, but it is not much consolation for someone currently coming to the end of a course of study that has not developed them. As one writer has put it

'Inspection and evaluation are in the same relationship to the daily learning experiences of the current generation of learners as the post-mortem is to preventative medicine.'

(West – Burnham, 1994)

So try to focus on 'preventative medicine' and plan to get things right first time, if at all possible, rather than waiting for inspectors to appear. Thereafter, ongoing evaluation will confirm whether your plans are working successfully or not. In that connection, you are referred back to the discussion of reality checking of plans that we had at the end of *Session 5* and are reminded of the importance of sharing ongoing evaluation with your colleagues.

Feedback WS6(b): How to evaluate

It is impossible to gain a fully valid insight into a person's teaching skills without actually watching their performance. So if a teacher is to have useful feedback on his or her abilities as a teacher then classroom observation must take place. Furthermore, discussion with colleagues and analysis of pupil performance is most constructive when linked with given classroom visits. There are, however, three major points to be emphasised, a couple of them quite controversial:

- The arrangements for observation should be agreed between the observer and the observed
- The observer need not have greater expertise than the observed
- In peer coaching, the observer should avoid providing feedback unless it is asked for

The latter two points may seem rather surprising but, as was noted in *Thought Piece B,* the work of Joyce and Showers on staff development strongly suggests that when teachers try to give each other feedback as a part of peer coaching, collaborative activity tends to disintegrate. This is especially the case when feedback is evaluative.

What is important is for peers to support growth in the quality of *self-reflection* in each other. After an observer watches an activity, (s)he needs to ask probing open-ended questions of a kind that will require the observed to reflect more deeply on what they were doing and why.

Research indicates that peer group coaching can help staff development despite, or perhaps because of the lack of feedback so long as three elements are present:

1. Participants know that no external evaluation will be employed unless they actively seek it
2. There are tools for self-reflection that participants find useful such as, for example the *Standard for Team Leadership, Quality Indicators* and, when a range of perspectives is being sought, the *360º review instrument* provided below.

3. Peers avoid expressions of judgment but focus rather on such techniques as pausing, paraphrasing, asking open-ended questions and providing data that allows their colleagues to draw their own conclusions.

Learning Rounds

The benefits of a non-judgemental, evidence-based approach to needs identification, followed by analytical discussion of needs as a means of beginning to meet them, have been most recently demonstrated in an initiative that is being led by the Scottish Centre for Studies in School Administration (SCSSA) with the support of the national CPD team and government backing.

Learning Rounds are so called after the idea of medical rounds where senior doctors are followed by students as they complete their rounds of wards and invite them to participate in a shared discussion of what the needs of patients might be and how they might be addressed.

Details vary but in essence Learning Rounds involve:

- A small group of colleagues observing an agreed aspect of the work of one of their number (with all being volunteers)
- The recording of a series of non-judgemental statements by the visitors about what they saw
- A discussion afterwards between the observers and the observed colleague where there is a focus on *joint discussion and reflection* upon perceptions about what happened— not the more traditional advice of the observer advising/telling the observed about what he/she must do to improve
- An opportunity for the *observed colleague* to draw up an action plan of next steps in terms of what he/she is going to do to build on current levels of competence in the area of focus, based on the shared discussions and reflections of what was observed
- An opportunity for further discussions between the observing group and the observed colleague to comment upon the proposed action plan before implementation
- An opportunity for rotation of roles within the group so that over time all observe and are observed

Clearly, Learning Rounds are linked to peer coaching of the kind that we have discussed and recommended earlier. So far they have been used to promote the kind of informed reflection on teaching practice that is the first step in improving that practice. But the same principles apply to evaluating leadership skills.

The sharing of draft action plans with colleagues that was recommended in Session 5 is a particularly good example of a peer coaching approach to one aspect of leadership development. Readers may be interested to note that this session of the programme, in which colleagues help each other to reflect on their planning skills, has consistently proved to be one of the most popular and successful sessions of the whole programme over the years. There is evidence to suggest that the planner's planning skills will improve if questions by the observer are probing enough to reveal where there is a lack of clarity of purpose and procedure in the original plan – even if the observer does not follow through with words of wisdom and advice about how the planner could indeed improve the plan.

Search for 'Learning Rounds' in Google for more information.

Look up www.scssa.ed.ac.uk for details of the national initiative.

Follow - up and support

The programme, 'Developing Excellent Team Leaders' comprises three elements:

a) Individually working through or attending workshop sessions on key leadership themes

b) Planning and leading the implementation of a school-based project

c) Compiling a reflective portfolio on the impact of the project on personal and school improvement.

Now that readers have completed the workshop activities and have hopefully gained some new insights into how to deal with the leadership challenges that may come their way, it is time for them to put their new or refreshed knowledge and understanding to the test by undertaking a school-based project whereby they will lead a small working party towards improving some aspect of provision, either at departmental level in the case of aspiring middle managers or at whole school level in the case of aspiring senior managers. As was noted earlier, drawing up an action plan and a personal learning plan is the first step in leading a school-based project and the activities of Session 5 are relevant here. The work of *Joyce and Showers* that we looked at in *Thought Piece B* consistently emphasises the importance of translating leadership theory into leadership practice, especially if the practice is supported by a coach or mentor. Hence the importance now of designing and implementing a school-based improvement plan as the next phase of the programme.

360º Review

Leadership requires courage. And one of the most courageous things leaders can do is to check their perception of their leadership qualities with the perceptions of others. This is self-evaluation with a vengeance.

A particularly useful way for you to evaluate your leadership skills is to conduct a *360° review* of what has become known as your emotional intelligence. The work of Daniel Goleman and others on emotional intelligence was discussed earlier and clearly such intelligence is essential for excellent leadership. The concept is closely linked to the Personal Qualities and Interpersonal Skills element of the Standard for Leadership that was introduced in workshop Session 1.

360º reviews involve your approaching various colleagues who know your work, one or two senior colleagues, one or two peers and one or two junior colleagues and inviting them to complete a detailed review of your emotional intelligence from their point of view. You might even invite opinions from support staff, parents and pupils, as well as self-evaluating.

Such a review would be the first and possibly most challenging step to take if you wish to develop your emotional intelligence. In this connection, it is worth noting that although people seem naturally to have such emotional intelligence in varying degrees, the various competences can be learned. Leaders can learn, for example, to develop empathy for the viewpoint of others. It would help you to identify the skills that you would like to develop in any project you might undertake. And it would certainly help you to assess your progress if you issue the review again at the end of your project.

Much would depend, of course, on the reliability and validity of any 360º review and the procedure provides valuable insights into how you are perceived as a leader if your colleagues are honest in their appraisal and you invite them to be so.

Readers who are interested in undertaking a full review of their emotional intelligence may Google the Emotional Competence Inventory (ECI) developed by the Hay Group and based upon the work of Daniel Goleman and Dr Richard Boyatzis.

Alternatively, they may choose to conduct a review of the qualities and interpersonal skills looked for in *The Standard for Leadership*. In this case, they could issue copies of the list of emotional competences listed below and invite colleagues to rate them in terms of current levels of competence.

Follow –up Activity

As part of the self-evaluation process, it is strongly recommended that readers should issue copies of the inventory of personal qualities and interpersonal skills that follows to the members of their project team before and after they have completed the school-based project. They may wish also to issue the inventory to at least two senior colleagues, two peers and two junior colleagues who are familiar with their work. The inventory is based on the qualities and interpersonal skills identified in the *Standard for Leadership* issued earlier.

Readers and their colleagues should provide ratings on each competence within the inventory by indicating the frequency with which they have observed the leader illustrating the competence in question. Use the following rating scale:

1: never observed; 2: seldom observed; 3: sometimes observed; 4: often observed; 5: consistently observed; 6: N/A: no opportunity to observe.

An Inventory of the Personal Qualities and Interpersonal Skills of Aspiring Leaders

Please rate the frequency with which the leader has illustrated the under noted skills, using the following code:
1: never observed; 2: seldom observed; 3: sometimes observed; 4: often observed; 5: consistently observed; 6: N/A: no opportunity to observe.

Demonstrating Self-Awareness:
- Recognises personal moods and their impact

- Keeps feelings under control

- Recognises personal strengths and needs

- Has a due measure of self-esteem

Inspiring and Motivating Others
- Calm in the face of challenges

- Acts with integrity by exemplifying stated values

- Sensitive to the feelings of others and helps them to manage them

- Understands and values other points of view

- Persistently promotes excellent standards

- Promotes a collegiate approach to dealing with agreed aims

- Negotiates and resolves disagreements

Judging Wisely and Deciding Appropriately
- Plans effective strategies and policies

- Uses a range of appropriate decision-making processes

- Responds flexibly to alternative ideas

- Builds on strengths and opportunities and reduces obstacles and threats

- Keeps decisions under review

Communicating Effectively
- Provides timely information

- Gives clear expression to ideas and personal values

- Is a good listener

- Invites and is open to feedback

- Demonstrates public relations skills

Showing Political Insight

- Understands and manages personal power and influence for the good of the community

- Can read and manage the power relationships within and between groups

- Understands and responds to the broader needs of society

Developing Excellent Team Leaders:
Guide to the Reflective Portfolio

Developing Excellent Team Leaders:
Guide to the Reflective Portfolio

Introduction

The Preface to this leadership development programme makes it clear that there are three key components in the structure of the programme:

(a) Working through a series of workshop sessions on key leadership themes

(b) Planning and leading the implementation of a school-based project

(c) Compiling a reflective portfolio of evidence of the project's impact on personal and school improvement.

All of these components are considered to be extremely important in helping readers to develop their leadership and management skills. The purpose of this short guide is to explain the rationale and the requirements of the *Reflective Portfolio.*

Rationale

As *Thought Piece A* from the programme materials makes clear, leaders learn through a process of experiential learning. A key aspect of such learning is the process of reflecting upon experience. Such reflection comprises a mixture of:

- direct personal thinking about leadership experience
- discussion with others about the nature and value of the experience
- reading about similar experiences and the learning that others gained
- analysis of the outcomes of leadership experience

The conclusions that you arrive at as a result of such reflection will influence the way in which you operate as a leader in future. There is particular value in writing up such reflections as a means of further clarifying your thinking—not to mention refining your written communication skills.

You have spent some time leading a school-based project that aimed to improve some aspect of learning and teaching and consequential pupil attainment or achievement even as you sought to improve your current leadership and management skills.

In the *Reflective Portfolio* you are invited to reflect upon that process in terms of *what* you did, *how* you went about it and *why* you acted as you did. In particular, you should provide any evidence that you have been able to accrue that demonstrates how your leadership has lead directly or indirectly to improved outcomes for learners.

The *Reflective Commentary* is in three parts, each around *1000-1200 words* in length.

Section A: Implementation of the project

Section B: Impact of the project

Section C: Dealing with particular challenges

Section A: Implementation of the Project

At an earlier stage of the development programme, you were invited to submit, and receive comment on, an action plan in which you laid out a rationale for your school-based project and your proposed implementation strategies.

In *Section A* of your reflective commentary you are invited to provide a narrative, telling the story, supported by evidence, of how the things that you planned actually turned out. It is useful to subdivide *Section A* into two parts:

1. A Claim for Leadership Competence
2. Implementation of New Approaches

1. Your focus here is on describing the processes and procedures that you initiated to achieve your objectives. What did you actually do, as project leader, to involve other people? How did you conduct meetings? Did timings go as planned or did you have to deal with unforeseen delays? What did you do to minimise the impact of such delays?

What did you do to identify and use necessary resources? What steps did you take to provide working party members with any necessary CPD? What steps did you take to secure commitment and agreement among colleagues and to build a team spirit? These are the kind of questions that will guide you in composing that part of *Section A* that tells the story of how you led and managed colleagues in the school-based project.

You should refer to appropriate evidence in the appendix in support of your claims. Suitable items of evidence will include minutes of meetings, memos/emails to colleagues, diary extracts if you kept one, records of how resources were used and comment on how CPD was provided (for more detail see later)

2. Moving on from how you led your team, you should provide a description of the extent to which, if at all, you and your team implemented new approaches to learning and teaching. It may be that you led some piloting of new approaches or materials in which case a description of how you implemented and monitored these new approaches is looked for (remembering that *monitoring* refers only to the steps you took to ensure that agreed procedures were indeed carried out) Again you should refer to relevant evidence in the appendix – minutes of agreements, memos to staff, records of classroom visits for example.

With some projects, it may be that most, if not all, of the available time was devoted to arriving at an agreed policy statement that is to be implemented next session. In such cases, you should describe the processes by which you arrived at the agreed policy statement, before providing detailed proposals as to how the new policy is to be implemented in the future.

An example of a completed *Section A* is provided separately.

Section B: Impact of the Project

The importance of evaluating the impact of an initiative on school development was strongly emphasised in the programme input (See *Session 6*). HMI have also confirmed in their latest report (Sept 2008) the importance of evaluating initiatives in terms of improving outcomes for learners. This section of your portfolio deals with such evaluation.

All too often, evaluation is carried out in a rather brief and superficial way. 'Ticking all the boxes' has become a popular phrase for such approaches. In fact, evaluation is a complex process, certainly when you are trying to evaluate the impact that your leadership has had on learning. It includes trying to carry out self-evaluation of your own development as a leader, evaluation of the extent to which you have contributed to the development of your colleagues, evaluation of the extent to which colleagues have in turn incorporated new methods and materials into their classroom practice and ultimately, of course, evaluation of the extent to which new methods and materials have led to a demonstrable improvement in pupil attainment and achievement.

There is too a time factor built into all of this insofar as it may be some time before the impact of a new approach can be fully assessed. Indeed it may be that when the time for submitting your reflective commentary comes along, you will not have been able to carry out a full evaluation of the impact of your work particularly with regard to pupil performance and attainment.

Nevertheless, and especially if there has been some piloting of new approaches, there should be some preliminary indications of how well new approaches are proceeding in terms of what is happening in the classroom, with regard both to teaching and learning. You should also indicate how you intend in the fullness of time to evaluate the impact of your work more extensively. In other words you should explain your overall evaluation *strategy*.

It should also be possible for you to conduct a preliminary evaluation of your own leadership development, at least in the areas specified in your personal learning plan, and the impact of that leadership on working party and other colleagues (Use of the 360º review document provided in *Session 6* of the course materials is strongly recommended here, especially if you can persuade colleagues to be honest in their evaluations of your interpersonal skills)

As always, you should refer to evidence in the appendix that supports your claims for making an impact. On this occasion it is probable that evidence will include completed surveys of the kind described in *Session 6* of the programme materials, accompanied where relevant by pieces of pupil work that indicate improved skills in the area of provision under focus. You are likely also to be looking at any evidence thrown up by a consideration of the 4 Quality Indicators listed in the latest HMI Report on improving outcomes for learners (QI: 1.1, 2.1, 5.3, 5.9)

Thus you might include evidence of improvement in pupil attainment or achievement statistics, photographs or examples of pupil work that show an improvement over previous efforts. An example of a completed *Section B* is provided separately.

A Note on Selecting Evidence

Reference has been made several times now to the importance of providing in an appendix evidence of the work you have done to lead improvements in learning and teaching. In deciding the kind of evidence to submit, you should consider the following criteria:

Relevance: Does the selected evidence illustrate the process you undertook - particularly your leadership and management of others?

Sufficiency: Do the pieces of evidence fit together and taken as a series demonstrate the full management process (audit, planning, implementation, monitoring and evaluation) that you led?

Authenticity: Do the pieces of evidence show that *you* were responsible for activity that was undertaken? In this connection, do remember that you are claiming competence as a leader and not as a follower.

Competence: Have you demonstrated successful outcomes? Here evidence of monitoring and evaluation is crucial.

Section C: Dealing with particular challenges

Overall, the third section of the portfolio relates to the *Why* of leadership. *Workshop Session 2* argued that the deep-seated values and attitudes of a person have the biggest impact on their performance rather than knowledge and skills – however important these may be. Yet values may exist at semi-conscious or sub-conscious levels and it is important to reflect consciously – and honestly – on the impact they may have on our leadership actions as a means of improving leadership behaviour. Conscious reflection on your values is the purpose of this final section of the reflective portfolio. Why did you act as you did in particular situations? What values were driving you? What was your thinking and where had it come from in terms of previous experience, advice or reading? And what did you learn as a result of any particular situation about how to behave next time around in a similar situation?

The style of writing is now *reflective* and *analytical*, rather than *narrative* and *descriptive*. And, for the sake of encouraging some depth of thinking, you are invited to reflect on just one critical incident, issue or learning situation as it related to any one of the five areas of management activity – managing learning and teaching, managing people, managing change, managing resources and building community, or indeed any mixture of these. You might structure this section of the portfolio as follows:

The context

A brief paragraph that sets the context for the reader in which the critical incident or learning situation occurred

The strategy

This is another brief paragraph in which you describe what your original intentions or hopes were and why.

The critical incident

Now you should explain what the nature of the critical incident or learning situation was, the steps you took to deal with it and the reasons why you chose those steps.

The 'critical incident' need not be some dramatic disaster. Rather it is a moment in time or an unfolding scenario that was very much a learning situation for you (It is like the critical incident analysis that you already explored in *Workshop Session 1* of the programme) Perhaps you unwittingly contributed to the problem; perhaps it was a completely unexpected situation that you had to overcome if your objectives were to be achieved. Perhaps you had to cope with a difficult colleague.

In reflecting on why you did what you did to resolve the situation, you should explain the ways in which decisions that you took were influenced by previous experience, personal values, wise advice from other colleagues and personal reading. This is a good opportunity to demonstrate how 'theory', at least in the shape of the experiences of others and background reading can influence practice and deepen one's understanding of at least one of the competences of leadership and management.

Conclusions

In the last part of this section of the portfolio, you should explain what the outcomes were both in terms of resolving the situation and in terms of valuable insights that you gained about how to act in future if a similar situation were to arise again – or perhaps how to act in future in order to prevent a similar situation arising in the first place. You are also invited to sum up overall the ways in which you think you have progressed as a leader as a result of undertaking this development programme, referring the reader again to any evidence that you would use to support your beliefs and assertions.

It is important to ensure that the bulk of this section of the portfolio is indeed reflective and analytical in style. Extended narrative or description, beyond what is necessary to clue the reader into the context, is not wanted.

An example of a completed *Section C* is provided separately.

By the time you have completed the three sections of your portfolio, you should have put together a very thorough claim for competence, suitably supported by evidence, of how you led your project to a successful conclusion in terms of improved pupil attainment and achievement and improved leadership practice.

As noted earlier, try to keep the length of each section to around 1000 - 1200 words. Universities usually accept a 10% margin either side of the recommended amount, exclusive of evidence. Provide evidence in a series of coded appendices but be selective there too.

And don't forget to supply a properly constructed bibliography (see further below)

It may be that you prefer to use tables, diagrams or bullet points partly to explain what you did and how you went about things, thus reducing the number of words used. This is perfectly acceptable so long as what you did and how you went about it is clear to the reader and permits of formative assessment of the kind indicated in the sample assessment proforma below. Similarly, you may reduce the length of Section C, so long as you make it clear *why* you chose to do the things that you did and *why* you believe overall that you have developed as a leader

Reflective Portfolio Assessment Criteria

For readers who choose to submit their reflective commentaries to a programme tutor, the portfolio will be assessed formatively on the basis of the following criteria:

- ✓ The ability to describe and evaluate practice effectively
- ✓ The ability to demonstrate professional development through critical reflection on experience
- ✓ The ability to demonstrate professional development through critical reflection on relevant reading
- ✓ The ability to provide a structured and coherent account of the work undertaken

Where readers prefer to submit their portfolios to their head teacher, it is suggested that the same criteria should be used.

Evidence of such formative assessment will be relevant to claims for formal recognition of leadership development from the GTCS, as will endorsements of the leadership development of teachers by their head teachers.

Presentation and Style of the Reflective Portfolio

One copy of the Reflective Portfolio should be submitted to the head teacher or programme tutor by the due date. Participants should also retain a copy.

There should be a front page that includes:

Name of Participant

School

Local Authority, where relevant

Contact Details, including address, phone number and email address

Title of project

Date of submission

There should be a contents page identifying the major sections of the commentary. Page numbers should be used throughout the commentary.

Materials where appropriate, should be presented on single sided A4 paper with an adequate margin. Font size 11 or 12 is recommended. If hand written, legible and well-spaced script should be used. An <u>accessible</u> folder or binding should be used.

All materials should be clearly structured using headings and subheadings as appropriate. All diagrams, charts or grids should be clearly labelled.

A full bibliography, in alphabetical order, should be included using the Harvard citation system:

For book: publisher	Author (date) title, place of publication,
	E.g. Leask, M and Terrell, I, (1997) *Development Planning and School Improvement for Middle Managers* London, Kogan Page.
For chapters (in an edited book):	Author (date) title in Editor(s) Title, place of publication, publisher, page numbers.
Teams in	e.g. O'Neill, J. (1997) *Managing Through*
	Bush, T and Middlewood, D. *Managing People In Education:* London, Paul Chapman, p 76-90.
For journal	Author (date) Title in Journal Title. Vol./Serial number, article: date, page numbers.
	E.g. Wise, C and Bush, T (1999) *From Teacher to Manager: The Role of the Academic Middle Manager in Secondary Schools* in *Educational Research* 41 (2) pp 183-196
For official of Publication,	Author/Organisation (date) Title, place

documents: Publisher.

e.g. SCCC (1995) *Teaching for Effective Learning*

Edinburgh, SCCC.

All quotes in the texts should use one of the following conventions:

Graham (1996 p. 38) argues that "School development planning offers a variety of approaches."

Within the framework of SDP a number of different approaches to planning are available (Graham, 1996).

All evidence should be labelled and an index/list of evidence included.

Where continuous prose is used, appropriate conventions are followed for spelling, punctuation, sentence structure and paragraphing.

Developing Excellent Team Leaders: Examples of Reflective Portfolios

Developing Excellent Team Leaders: Examples of Reflective Portfolios

Introduction

What follows are examples of reflective portfolios submitted by previous participants in this leadership development programme. Examples of each section have been taken from three different portfolios. Evidence, although alluded to, is not included to preserve confidentiality.

Section A: Implementation of the Project

1. A Claim for Leadership Competence

I was invited by the head teacher to lead a small group looking into the application of, and the effectiveness of, the current behaviour policy in the school and to make recommendations for implementing an improved policy. Staff had been complaining that pupil behaviour was at its worst ever, with constant referrals about disruptive behaviour. Indeed there had been a 34% increase in referrals over the last two years. Parents had also been complaining about an increase in bullying and wanted to know what the school was doing about it. Absence and late-coming figures were on the increase and I shared the concern of the head teacher that there were serious issues to be addressed, not least the impact on pupil attainment and achievement

My first step was to issue a memo inviting volunteers to join me in this initiative and setting a date for the first meeting of the group (Item 1, memo to staff).The initial response was not very good and it did not look as if I would get the kind of representative group that I was looking for. I approached one or two people personally whom I thought might be interested and eventually managed to persuade two additional members to join up, making a total of five including myself. In the event I was very pleased because the group was representative in their views, ranging from those who were keen on a more positive approach to pupil behaviour to one in particular who tended to be of the 'hang-them-high' brigade. At the first meeting of the group I shared with the other members the draft plan (Item 2, draft plan) that I had drawn up with a view to overtaking the requirement. Two members thought that the plan was rather ambitious but thought that it was worth proceeding to see how things would go. I suggested that our first step as a group was to carry out a detailed audit of existing practice and attitudes towards behaviour management and this was agreed (Item 3, minute of first meeting) One of the group issued a questionnaire to staff on current practice and attitudes that we as a group drew up (Item 4, staff questionnaire). Meanwhile I spoke to the pupil council and to a sample of parents about their attitudes to current practices (Item 5, notes from interviews) As a group we drew up a summary of our findings and discussed them at our next meeting (Items 6, 7, summary of findings and minute of meeting)

My next step was to continue with the agreed series of meetings of the group where we could plan a new approach to promoting better behaviour, based on our summary findings from the audit of current practice. In particular I was keen to move towards a system where the focus was on encouraging good behaviour through a system of rewards rather than on a system of punishments. I suggested that the group should make itself familiar with the SEED document, Better Behaviour –Better Learning and I undertook to visit a local school that had already moved to a new system, apparently with some success. I also arranged that one of the group could attend a one-day course on promoting positive behaviour (Items 8,9,10 minutes of meetings and brief report of school visit) and report back to the others (Item 11, conference report)

Between September and December we were able to meet three times for an hour each at the end of the school day to discuss our unfolding proposals (see Minutes 12(a), (b), (c) A further meeting at the end of December had to be cancelled when the school was closed because of bad weather but I took the chance to chat to each member of the group informally about how they felt the new proposed behaviour policy document was shaping up. The proponent of a sanctions approach was still unconvinced of the value of the proposals that the group were making concerning a more positive approach but had been impressed enough with the views of a friend in another school where such an approach was already in place to give grudging support to the group.

By the end of January I was able to draw up a draft policy statement on promoting better behaviour based upon the various views that had been expressed and presented this, first to the group and then to the staff in general as being worthy of piloting with one class. I then drew up a final draft in line with suggestions that came back (Item 13(a), first draft, item 13(b), summary comments, item 14, and final draft).

2. Implementation of new approaches

I then began to implement the new approach with the specified class, working with and through the classroom teacher. I made arrangements to visit the class once a week to see how things were progressing (Item 15, record of class visits)

Shortly after Easter I had a meeting with the classroom teacher to evaluate the impact of the new approach to behaviour on classroom discipline and on numbers of behaviour referrals (Item 16, record of meeting and relevant statistics) Another member of the group interviewed children and some parents about their views about what improvements had come about, if any (Item 17, record of views)

At the next meeting of the group in late April I brought the group up to date on my findings from the pilot and discussions with the classroom teacher and my colleague reported on the favourable views coming from the children and their parents. We then discussed as a group what should be proposed to the head teacher with regard to finalising a new behaviour policy for general implementation in the new term (Item 18, minutes of meeting and Behaviour Policy Statement) I also invited the group to evaluate their own involvement in the group and my leadership of it (Item19) using the 360º appraisal document. Details are in the next section.

At the time of writing, it is intended to roll out the new policy at the start of Session 2009 – 2010. It is likely that the various members of the group will be focusing on new priorities but I have been invited by the head teacher to continue to monitor and evaluate the progress of the new policy as it becomes embedded in school practice. I intend to carry out a full survey of impact with all staff, pupils and parents in late October, 2010. (1087 words)

Section B: Impact of the project

It was my aim to improve the standard of ICT provision in the Department for S1 and S2 pupils, thus in turn improving pupil progress through increased use of programmes in literacy. From initial discussions so far (See diary note, Item B1) and from working with the project, I can see that providing a structure that meets the 5-14 requirements of ICT is providing continuity and progression in lessons and programmes of study. Colleagues have commented that in the past they were unclear about what to teach and now they have clear guidelines and expectations about what their pupils should be learning (See Item B2, staff comments)

I realise, however, that to evaluate the full impact of this project, it will need to be operational for a full school session. Evaluations next session will be carried out on a more formal basis and I would expect to have further meetings with staff to establish expectations, evaluate methods for next session and to evaluate actual progress in pupil attainment. A true picture of the success of the programme will only be gained at the end of session when the new S1 class will have completed S2. Information will also be sought from S3 teachers at that point to see if they have noticed a change in the abilities of the new former S2 cohort in terms of using computers and benefiting in terms of attainment accordingly.

When planning this project, I based the proposed evaluation on certain Quality Indicators from 'How Good Is Our School'. By using these QIs I have realised that although we have achieved a lot, there is still room for improvement. QI 1.2 deals with course and programmes, partly in terms of continuity and progression. I know that this project now provides continuity and progression between S1 and S2 because we are closely covering 5-14 and skills are being built upon and not duplicated (See the new planners, Items B3 and B4) 6.3 deals with planning of teachers and through the establishment of the new planners, teachers can be sure that they are meeting 5-14 requirements.

In the beginning I also based this project on QI 5.3, meeting pupils' needs. Through discussion with colleagues I realised that an element of differentiation needs to be built into planners, not only for children struggling and needing consolidation but for children needing extension work to stretch their skills. This will need to be addressed when the working party resumes next session.

I feel that there are other ways in which I have benefited from this project. I undertook the Leadership course at the start of my first year as a principal teacher. It was beneficial to have a framework to follow to allow me to lead the project. Through leading a small group I gained confidence in addressing colleagues and in trying to motivate them in connection with something that was important to me. I also saw the importance of using the skills and knowledge of others and attaching value to this. The concept of planning and managing change was new to me and it certainly helped to have a clear project plan with initial time scales – even although I had to make a number of adjustments as time went by and unforeseen complications of the type that I described in Section A arose. I shall be reflecting one particular critical incident in Section C of this Commentary. The list of points below indicates how I felt I have progressed generally as a leader.

Leadership Development

1. Plan and lead a project:

I successfully set up and led a small group, planned and conducted useful meetings, monitored and evaluated initial success

2. Decision making skills

I was willing to change the focus of the original plan after discussion with colleagues and made good use of resources after liaising with the head teacher about how to use the budget

3. Ability to evaluate current practice and published material

I evaluated existing materials for S2 and decided which parts to retain. I issued or prepared new materials for S1 throughout the project

4. Motivational Skills

I secured the commitment of the team to the success of the project but was conscious that I was devoting much more time to it than they could afford, given their other commitments

5. Communication skills

I increased in confidence in chairing meetings and setting agendas. I learned the value of transparency when facing problems

6. Sensitivity to colleagues

I recognised that this project was 'my baby' and that I had to be careful about how much I asked of others in terms of their workload. I also realised that it was perfectly possible for any one of the team to come with better ideas than me about how to do things

The table is based upon my original Personal Learning Plan and the evidence to support my views comes largely from the 360º appraisals that were completed by team members and analysed by me (See Item B6)

So far as the other members of the group are concerned, they felt that they have had a particularly good opportunity to learn more about the use of ICT in promoting learning. They were also pleased to be part of planning and implementing this project and are keen to continue next year. (See group survey of views, Item B7) (901 words)

Section C: Dealing with particular challenges

Context
As described earlier in Section A, the HMI Report on our school stated as one of the main points of action:

'With a view to raising attainment, the head teacher should extend the system for monitoring the work of the school to include more focused visits to classrooms and a more frequent sampling of pupil's work'.

My head teacher readily acknowledged that it was important to encourage a high quality consistency of approach among all staff.

At the same time, she appreciated that the whole idea of direct monitoring through classroom observation was a very sensitive issue. She felt strongly that it was essential to secure the commitment of the whole staff to any new monitoring practices. Accordingly she invited me to put together a small representative working party to look at the issue and make proposals to her.

Strategy

I agree with Leask and Terrell, when they say:

'In particular, we highlight the importance for the middle manager to understand the different beliefs and values held by staff, and how these influence the way they approach their work. We also emphasise the importance of adopting a style of leadership and management appropriate to the individual context of the institution.'

(Development Planning and School Improvement for Middle Managers (1997), p 128)

I also agree with all those commentators (including my head teacher) who declare that the best way of securing the commitment of staff to implementing a new initiative is to involve them in formulating the initiative in the first place. With that in mind, I invited the staff to nominate three representatives to serve on the working party, one from each stage of the school. My intention was to start off with whatever their views were on monitoring and evaluation and to work from there.

Critical Incident

I was taken aback at the first meeting of the group to discover the strength of antagonism among the group members towards the idea of more formal monitoring. In essence they saw it as a kind of spying in order to blame teachers when things went wrong and results were not good enough. They felt the whole business would be a time-consuming paper exercise that would cut into valuable teaching time (See the minutes of the meeting, Item 2 in the appendix)

Personally, I was strongly convinced of the desirability of having an effective policy on self-evaluation .It seemed to me essential that we all needed to have a thorough and objective review of our current strengths as a first step to building on them. The challenge was to secure a similar level of commitment from the working group of volunteers. I began to appreciate the validity of O'Neill's definition of a team as:

'A small group of people who recognize the need for constructive conflict when working together in order for them to make, implement and support workable decisions.'

(In Managing People in Education, edited by Bush and Middlewood, 1997, pp 78-79)

But what was I going to do to resolve this conflict – or at least make it constructive?

Then the thought occurred to me that that we were coming from two different ends – they thought of external spies, I thought of self-evaluation; they thought of looking for weaknesses and I thought of looking for strengths; they thought the focus would be on teacher input and I accepted that the focus should be on pupil outcomes. It was also becoming obvious to me that the members of the group were not really all that clear about the basic meaning of monitoring and evaluation. Indeed there was not even an understanding of the difference in meaning between the two terms.

I agree with Fullan (1992) that leaders can increase their effectiveness by giving staff responsibilities through empowerment. But teachers need knowledge and understanding of the issues as well. Pooled ignorance is not a basis for effective decision- making. Perhaps if the group members had the chance to read the documents and extracts that I had been reading on the value of monitoring and evaluation then they would be more inclined to agree with me about the value of these processes.

It had been my intention to begin our work by working with the group to draw up a staff questionnaire on existing school practice with regard to school self-evaluation but I now suggested that we needed more discussion about our own respective views first. I would put together a package of key documents and extracts on the topic of monitoring and evaluation (See the appendix, Item 3, for the list in question) for the group to read in advance of the next meeting.

Our second meeting (See Item 4, the minutes of the meeting in the appendix) was entirely devoted to what in effect was their development. Most of them had read the material I had prepared and most were pleasantly surprised to discover the developmental emphasis that underpinned the approach recommended in the materials. They were also delighted to realise that, albeit perhaps in informal ways, they were already practising a range of methods for monitoring and evaluation, and had been for years. We had an excellent discussion, at the end of which the group were able to agree that it was meaningless to talk of supporting colleagues without suitably sensitive observation of their work and suitably sensitive discussion with them about what their needs and the needs of their pupils actually were.

What was most important was that we were able to agree that blaming and criticising were a destructive use of the processes of monitoring and evaluation and a negation of their true value. Through a process of rigorous self-evaluation, making use of a wide range of instruments that were readily available in, for example, How Good Is Our School, teachers would be able to identify their needs more clearly and could be supported more relevantly. The emphasis on support was essential and pupils would be the beneficiaries.

But at least, after all that reading and discussion, the working party accepted as a team what the key elements of a policy on self-evaluation might be and how they might work together to persuade the staff of its value. We had moved fairly rapidly through the stages of forming, storming and norming – and could begin performing! (See Law and Glover, Educational Leadership and Learning, p 75)

Conclusions

I learned a couple of valuable lessons from that first meeting. One was to realise that to start with where your colleagues were rather than where you would like them to be was essential. I also realised just how important it was to encourage informed opinion among people by ensuring that they had access to relevant reading that would enhance their knowledge and understanding of issues. It had not really occurred to me before that shared reading was one way of 'fostering a sense of shared purpose' (Everard and Morris, 2006)

By organising a reading pack on monitoring and evaluation, I believe that I had helped to turn the group into more of a team with:
- Shared perceptions
- A common purpose
- Agree procedures
- Commitment
- Cooperation
- Resolving disagreements by discussion

(Bell, Managing Teams in Secondary Schools, 1992)

Certainly some of the comments in the 360° appraisals from group members (See Item 10 in the appendix) would seem to bear that out.

From then on we worked steadily away at our meetings to develop a draft policy on self-evaluation that has now been introduced to all staff. There is no doubt that the willingness of the staff representatives to support it is encouraging other staff to change their minds too.

Once all staff views have received further consideration, I anticipate that we shall introduce the policy at the start of next session. It has been agreed that the working of the policy will be kept under review and that it will be adapted as required.

My head teacher seems delighted!

I have already described in Section B, with supporting evidence, the benefits I believe I have had from my involvement in this development programme. In future I think I would like to learn even more about some of the topics that were dealt with in individual sessions—such as negotiation skills and dealing with difficult people.

(1386 words)

Further reading for aspiring middle and senior managers

An important part of the team leadership programme is private reading. The various thought pieces provided throughout the programme are intended as a starter in this respect. They are, however, edited in line with the author's own views and it is important to consider a number of perspectives on any given leadership issue. In this connection, the under noted texts have proved to be popular with previous aspiring middle managers. A number of them include very readable overviews of the topics in focus. The list on the next page might be more appropriate for aspiring senior managers, although all the texts listed could be of value to either category of reader. Downloadable materials and the addresses of some popular websites are also included.

Brundrett, M and Terrell, I (2004) *Learning to Lead in the Secondary School: Becoming an Effective Head of Department:* Routledge Falmer

Bush, T. and Middlewood, D. (eds.) (2005) *Leading and Managing People in Education*: Paul Chapman

Dean, J (2003) *Subject Leadership in the Primary School: A Practical Guide for Curriculum Coordinators:* David Fulton

Everard, B. Morris, G. Wilson, I (2004) *Effective School Management*: Paul Chapman

Fleming, Peter (2000) *The Art of Middle Management in Secondary Schools*: David Fulton

Fleming, Peter (2001) *The Art of Middle Management in Primary Schools*: David Fulton

Harris, A and Muijs,D (2004) *Improving Schools Through Teacher Leadership:* Open University Press

Kydd. L. Anderson, L. and Newton, W. (2003) *Leading People and Teams in Education*: Paul Chapman

Law, S. and Glover, D. (2000) *Educational Leadership and Learning*: Open University Press

Leask, M and Terrell, I (1997) *Development Planning and School Improvement for Middle Managers:* Kogan Page

MacGilchrist, B, Reed, J. and Myers, K. (2004) *The Intelligent School*: Paul Chapman

McLean, A (2003) *The Motivated School:* Paul Chapman

Further reading for aspiring senior managers

Bennett, N., Crawford, M and Cartwright, M (eds) (2002) *Effective Educational Leadership*: London: Paul Chapman

Bowring-Carr, C and West-Burnham, J (1997) *Effective Learning in Schools: How to Integrate Learning and Leadership for a Successful School*: London: Pitman Publishing

Brighouse, T. and Woods, D. (1999) *How to Improve Your School*: London: Routledge

Bush, T and Bell, L (eds) (2002) *The Principles and Practice of Educational Management:* London: Paul Chapman

Day, C., Hall, C. And Whitaker, P (1998) *Developing Leadership in Primary Schools*: London: Paul Chapman

Everard, K.B., Morris, G. and Wilson, I (2004) *Effective School Management*: London: Paul Chapman

Fidler, B. (2002) *Strategic Management for School Development*: London: Paul Chapman

Fullan, M and Hargreaves, D (1991) *What's worth fighting for in your school?* Buckingham: Open University Press

Harris, A and Lambert, L (2003) *Building Leadership Capacity for School Improvement*: Maidenhead: Open University Press

Kydd. L. Anderson, L. and Newton, W. (2003) *Leading People and Teams in Education*: Paul Chapman

Law, S. And Glover, D. (2000) *Educational Leadership and Learning: Practice, Policy and Research*: Buckingham: Open University Press

MacBeath, J and Myers, K. (1999) *Effective School Leadership*: Hemel Hempstead: Prentice Hall

MacGilchrist, B.,Myers, K., and Reed, J. (2004) *The Intelligent School* (2nd edition) London: Sage Publications

McLean, A (2003) *The Motivated School:* Paul Chapman

O'Brien, J., Murphy, D. And Draper, J (2008) *School Leadership;* Edinburgh: Dunedin

Preedy, M., Glatter,R.and Wise, C (2002) *Strategic Leadership and Educational Improvement*: London: Paul Chapman

Reeves, J., Forde, C., O'Brien, J, Smith, P, and Tomlinson, H. (2002) *Performance Management in Education: Improving Practice*: London: Paul Chapman

Southworth, G (1998) *Leading Improving Primary Schools*: London: Falmer Press

Tomlinson, H, Gunter, H and Smith, P (eds)(1999) *Living Headship: Voices, Values and Vision*: London: Paul Chapman

Tomlinson, H. (2004) *Educational Leadership*: London: Kogan Page

The following materials can be downloaded:

Note: If copying and pasting URLS into your browser does not work, search Google for titles and updated URLs

1. A range of evaluation tools in the *Journey to Excellence* Zone, including *How Good Is Our School? Self- Evaluation Using Quality Indicators*.

The site also provides very useful reports on school leadership, for example *Leadership for learning: The Challenges of leading in a time of change* (2007) *Improving outcomes for learners through self-evaluation* (2008) *Learning Together: Lessons about school improvement* (2009)

www.hmie.gov.uk

2. Continuing Professional Development for Educational Leaders

www.scotland.gov.uk/library5/education/cpdel.pdf
3. The Standard for Headship

www.scotland.gov.uk/Publications/2005/11/3085829/58300

4. The Leadership Toolkit: Readings on Key Leadership Topics

http://www.ltscotland.org.uk/cpdscotland/cpdfind/oppdetails.asp?inst=1143

5. The EIS and Leadership in Schools: Policy Paper (2008)

http://www.eis.org.uk

Websites

http://www.ltscotland.org.uk/cpdscotland - for a wide range of advice and support for your continuing professional development

www.scotland.gov.uk/library - for all sorts of SEED publications

www.ltscotland.org.uk/curriculumfor excellence/ - the main site for all aspects of the Curriculum for Excellence

www.hmie.gov.uk - read what the inspectors have to say about leadership and management in primary and secondary school inspection reports (as well as in the reports mentioned earlier)

www.scre.ac.uk - to pick up on a range of short and readable research reports in the Spotlight and Interchange series

www.ltscotland.com - to find out about a range of issues relating to learning and teaching, not least in relation to 'A Curriculum for Excellence' and materials related to Assessment Is For Learning

www.nationalcollege.org.uk - website of the English National College for School Leadership, with an extensive range of articles and recommendations on school leadership

www.gtcs.org.uk- especially useful for information on the Scheme of Recognition

www.google.com - if you can't find it, type it in and ask 'Google' to search for it. Type in 'school leadership' for a lifetime of fascinating reading.

Developing Excellent Team Leaders: Evaluation

This leadership development programme has evolved over several years in line with evaluation comments from readers and programme participants and new perspectives on leadership. New readers and participants are cordially invited to contribute to future editions of the programme and book by completing the form below and emailing it to dlynas22@aol.com

Please evaluate the workshop sessions, using a six-point rating system:

6= excellent; 5= very good; 4= good; 3= satisfactory; 2= weak; 1= unsatisfactory

Clarity of Preface

Usefulness of Thought Pieces

Value of workshop sessions in terms of:

       Range of leadership topics covered

       Nature of activities

       Input by leadership coach/peer coaches

       Relevance to stated learning outcomes

       Relevance to personal leadership development

Venue (if applicable)

Please comment briefly on any workshop sessions that were particularly useful to you

Please indicate ways in which any workshop sessions could be improved

Please indicate how you feel you might benefit personally from your involvement in this programme

Please indicate how you feel your school might benefit from your involvement in this programme

Name: Date:

Lightning Source UK Ltd.
Milton Keynes UK
29 March 2011

170050UK00001B/7/P